Teach the Way
They Learn

Teach the Way They Learn

62 Easy,
Engaging & Effective
Language-Arts
Activities

BY JOANNE I. HINES & PAMELA J. VINCENT

Crystal Springs
BOOKS

A division of **SDE** Staff Development for Educators

Peterborough, New Hampshire

Published by Crystal Springs Books
A division of Staff Development for Educators (SDE)
10 Sharon Road, PO Box 500
Peterborough, NH 03458
1-800-321-0401
www.crystalsprings.com
www.sde.com

Published 2005

Printed in the United States of America

09 08 07 06 05   1 2 3 4 5

ISBN: 1-884548-72-5

Library of Congress Cataloging-in-Publication Data

Hines, Joanne I., 1955-

   Teach the way they learn : 62 easy, engaging & effective language arts activities / by Joanne I. Hines & Pamela J. Vincent.

      p. cm.

   Includes index.

   ISBN 1-884548-72-5

   1. Language arts (Elementary)--Activity programs. I. Vincent, Pamela J., 1947- II. Title.

   LB1576.H514 2005

   372.6--dc22

                          2005007539

Editor: Sharon Smith

Creative Director, Designer, and Production Coordinator: Soosen Dunholter

Illustrator: Patrick Vincent

To my incredible children—Christal, Patrick, and Mikell—who are my toughest critics and yet my greatest fans! I love you "big as the sky!"

—Pam Vincent

To my wonderful husband, Bill, and my amazing sons, Craig and Willie. Your love and encouragement inspire me. I would not be who I am without you.

—Joanne Hines

Contents

Acknowledgments

We would like to acknowledge our dynamite editor, Sharon Smith, for her sense of humor, constant support, and never-ending perseverance; and our Art Director, Soosen Dunholter, for applying her wonderful creativity to the design of this book.

We would like to thank Lorraine Walker and her staff at Crystal Springs Books for believing in us and in our ideas.

Thank you, too, to Patrick Vincent for making the pages come alive with his illustrations.

Finally, we would like to thank all of the teachers and the students we have worked with over the years.

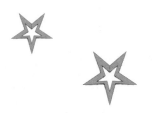

Skills Addressed & Suggested Grade Levels

	Vocabulary Development	Reading Comprehension	Language Skills	Working with Words	Spelling	Primary (K–3)	Intermediate (4–6)
Picture What You'll Read	★	★		★		★	★
Think Inside the Box	★		★	★		★	★
Make a Note of It	★	★	★			★	★
You're It	★			★		★	
Word Diary	★		★	★	★	★	★
Boogie Bugs	★		★			★	
Fast Flashlight Focus	★		★	★		★	
3-D Delight	★			★		★	
Partners on Parade	★		★			★	
Gimme a Break!	★	★	★	★		★	★
Red Light, Green Light	★		★	★		★	
You've Got Mail	★			★		★	
Bright Idea	★		★	★		★	
SODA Hunt	★	★	★			★	★
Lit Logs	★	★				★	★
Story Sacks	★	★	★			★	★
Story Sandwich		★	★			★	★
Ask, Ask Away!		★	★			★	★
Predict/React Journal		★	★			★	★
Memory Boosters		★	★			★	★
Frame a Story		★	★			★	★
Just Because			★	★		★	
Shirt Tales		★				★	★
Have a Ball with Questions		★	★			★	★
Mask a Character		★	★			★	
The Main-Idea Hand		★	★			★	★
Compound Cut-Up Choo Choo	★		★	★	★	★	★
Luscious Lollipops	★		★	★	★	★	★
Short Vowel Circle Sort			★	★	★	★	
ABCs if You Please		★	★	★		★	
Race-Car Speedway	★		★	★			
Crazy Context Clues	★	★	★			★	★

	Vocabulary Development	Reading Comprehension	Language Skills	Working with Words	Spelling	Primary (K–3)	Intermediate (4–6)
Author Map			★			★	★
Extra! Extra! Read All About It!		★	★			★	★
The Powerful Apostrophe			★	★	★	★	
Presentation Helpers			★			★	★
ABCs on the Go			★	★	★	★	
Describing Details with Diamonds	★	★	★			★	★
Goal Bracelet	★			★	★	★	★
What s in a Name?	★		★			★	★
Fun Fan	★			★	★	★	★
Word-Nas-Tics	★		★	★	★	★	★
Show Me	★		★	★		★	
Towels for Vowels	★		★	★	★	★	
Beanie Boosters	★		★	★	★	★	
Flip a Word	★	★	★	★	★	★	★
Step on It!			★	★	★	★	
We See Spots			★	★	★	★	
Quizboard	★		★	★	★	★	★
Shh! It s a Secret			★		★		★
Five Fabulous Phonics Minutes	★		★	★	★	★	★
Spelling Bingo	★		★	★	★	★	★
Royal Spellers				★	★	★	
Riddle Sticks	★		★	★	★	★	★
Circle Spelling				★	★	★	★
Stair-Step Spellers			★	★	★	★	★
Basketball Spelling				★	★	★	★
Echo Spelling				★	★	★	★
Using Your Noodle for Spelling				★	★	★	★
Matchbook Spelling	★		★	★	★	★	★
Puzzle Power			★	★	★	★	
Buddies for Study			★	★	★	★	★

Introduction

Teach the Way They Learn is a book we think you'll love to teach from and learn with for many years to come. It's designed for the teacher who's dedicated to teaching and who goes beyond the text to reach all students. In this book you'll find activities that are creative and brain based. They're techniques we've used successfully in our own classrooms for years; we've chosen them specifically because they're designed to engage a diverse range of students.

We've selected these particular activities for another reason, too. Each focuses on one or more important aspects of language arts: vocabulary, comprehension, language development, working with words, and/or spelling. If you need a quick idea to build student skills in any of these areas, take a look at the table on pages 12–13, which will show you which activities are designed to build which skills, and will also give you broad guidelines for grade ranges. Once you've identified something that seems likely to meet your needs, turn to that activity for a brief description, a note on when you might want to use it, the approximate group size and grade range for which it's appropriate, and a more specific note on its focus. (These are just suggestions, of course; you're the best judge of which activities are appropriate for your students.) You'll also find a list of materials and a description of any preparation required.

For the most part, we've tried to concentrate on activities that require little (if any) prep time and few materials beyond those basics available in most classrooms. After all, we're educators, too, and we know you don't have a lot of time or money for special materials.

We also know that many activities designed for reading development can be equally useful, with only minor adaptations, in other areas of the curriculum. For that reason, we've included variations with virtually every activity. We hope you'll find these ideas useful in all areas of your teaching.

Above all, our goal is to provide you with some fresh options to re-energize your students and give them that "I-can't-wait-to-get-to-school!" attitude we all so fervently welcome in our students. We believe *Teach the Way They Learn* will do exactly that.

Picture What You'll Read

This interactive strategy introduces the student to the characters and/or the setting, as well as the vocabulary of a story. It's particularly effective for acquainting students with the main characters before they read a story. It's also a great equalizer, because even the poorest reader can be successful and can develop prior knowledge about the story.

MATERIALS

Crayons or markers

1 piece of 12" X 18" white drawing paper for each student

1 piece of white poster board

STEP BY STEP

☆ Give each student one piece of drawing paper, along with crayons or markers.

☆ Explain to students that you and the class will be working together on this activity. You'll be using poster board and markers (or the chalkboard and colored chalk) for your part; they'll be completing their own versions of the activity at the same time, using the paper and crayons or markers.

☆ While students do the same thing on their papers, draw a border roughly 1 to 1 ½" in from the outer edge of the poster board, making it look like a frame.

☆ Talk to the class about the main characters in the story. As you talk, start drawing a picture of those characters.

☆ Have students draw as you draw.

☆ Add a few interesting details from the story to pique student curiosity.

☆ Introduce difficult vocabulary words from the story and write them around the edge of the paper, just outside the frame. If you include verbs, be careful to use the same verb tense that's used in the story.

☆ Ask students to write the same words on their papers.

☆ To keep students from being distracted while reading the story, collect all papers.

VARIATIONS

Use the same procedure but focus on the setting rather than the characters.

After reading the story, return students' drawings to them. Have them add details based on what they've learned in the story.

GRADES: 1–6
GROUP SIZE: whole group, with students working individually

WHEN TO USE: before reading
FOCUS: introducing characters & vocabulary

Think Inside the Box

Working with a simple grid, students create their own personal connections to help them remember vocabulary words.

MATERIALS

Grid reproducible (see page 19)

Plain white copier paper

Pencils

PREPARATION

Make one copy of the reproducible for each student and hand out the copies.

STEP BY STEP

☆ The student writes one vocabulary word in each of the six sections.

☆ The student thinks of an association he can make for each word, then goes to the little box in the corner of each section and writes or draws something to represent that association. If the word is "night," the student might draw a picture of a moon, or he might write "fight" or "sight." What the student puts in the box should be something that will help him to remember the word.

☆ Students discuss their associations with the class, further reinforcing their understanding of the words.

> ## FOR EXAMPLE
>
> A vocabulary association can be:
>
> an illustration
>
> a rhyming word
>
> a configuration of the word
>
> a similar word
>
> sounds in a word
>
> the word family the word belongs to
>
> anything else that will help the student to remember the word

VARIATIONS

For older students, include nine words rather than six.

Have the class decide together on the associations.

To encourage parent involvement, turn this into a homework assignment, asking students and parents to make connections together.

GRADES: *1–6*

GROUP SIZE: *individual*

WHEN TO USE: *before reading*

FOCUS: *vocabulary association & recognition*

Make a Note of It

Students work in pairs and use sticky notes to practice vocabulary-word recognition, question formulation, and story comprehension.

MATERIALS

1 sheet of plain paper for each student

6 sticky notes for each student

Pencils

STEP BY STEP

☆ Pair off students.

☆ Give each student one sheet of plain paper and six sticky notes.

☆ Ask each student to arrange two rows of sticky notes on her paper, with three sticky notes in each row.

☆ Ask her to write one vocabulary word from the story, or one question about the story, on each sticky note.

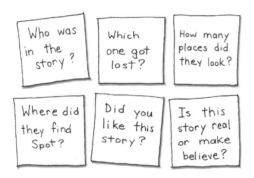

☆ Have her write her name at the top of the paper.

☆ Ask partners to exchange papers.

☆ Direct each student to lift each of her partner's sticky notes and to write under the sticky note a definition for the vocabulary word, a sentence using the vocabulary word, or an answer to the question. Explain that students should not remove the sticky notes.

☆ Ask each partner to write her name at the bottom of the paper on which she's responded to the sticky notes, then return the paper to her partner.

☆ Discuss questions and answers with the entire class.

VARIATIONS

Use this activity for content areas, asking students to write dates, names of important people, or place names on the sticky notes. In these cases, each partner writes under the sticky note an event that happened on that date, what that person is known for, or what's important about that place.

Have students scramble their spelling words and then write them on the sticky notes. Ask the partners to unscramble the words.

GRADES: *2–6*

GROUP SIZE: *pairs*

WHEN TO USE: *after reading*

FOCUS: *vocabulary development, question formulation & comprehension*

You're It

Students interact as they "become" the vocabulary words in this fast-paced, action-packed word-review game.

MATERIALS

List of vocabulary words (1 word per student)

1 large index card for each student

Marker

Hole punch

1 piece of yarn, 20 inches long, for each card

PREPARATION

Write one vocabulary word on each card. Punch two holes near the top corners of each card and attach the yarn, creating a "word bib." The bibs free students' hands for interaction with classmates.

STEP BY STEP

☆ Hand out the word bibs. Have students put on their bibs and stand in a circle. Explain that each student is to "become" his word; when you include the word "house" in your instructions, then the student with the "house" bib should respond to those instructions.

☆ Allowing time for the class to practice each step the first time around, give instructions that go something like this:

"Say your word as we go around the circle."

"When I say your word, turn around once and clap your hands."

"Listen for your word and follow directions. For example, if I say that 'star' should change places with 'house,' the two students wearing those word bibs should trade places." (Continue until all students have changed places.)

"Let's shake our words. For example, if I ask 'planet' and 'because' to shake, the students wearing those bibs should shake hands." (Continue until you've used all the words.)

"Listen and follow my directions. For example, if I say 'city' should stand between 'snow' and 'brown,' then the student wearing the 'city' bib should move to stand between the students wearing the 'snow' and 'brown' bibs." (Continue until all students have moved.)

"Give a high five. For example, if I ask 'better' to give a high five to 'snack,' the student wearing the 'better' bib should give a high five to the student wearing the 'snack' bib." (Continue until all students have participated.)

"If you are a noun, jump once." "If you are a verb, stoop down." "If you have a long vowel, clap your hands." "If you end with 'ing,' turn around." (Continue reviewing any skills and concepts you have previously taught.)

"Stand in alphabetical order. For example, if I call on 'star,' 'because,' and 'city' to stand in alphabetical order, the students wearing those words should come to the center of the circle and line up in alphabetical order." (Continue naming words until all students are in alphabetical order.)

☆ After the first round of practice, use this activity on a regular basis to review new vocabulary words.

VARIATION

With kindergarten students, use letters or numerals in place of words.

GRADES: *K–3*

GROUP SIZE: *4–12 students, or up to half the class*

WHEN TO USE: *before & after reading*

FOCUS: *vocabulary recognition & association*

Word Diary

By creating a four-part personal diary entry for a difficult word, a student can make the connections he needs to master vocabulary.

MATERIALS

Word diary reproducible (see page 23)

Plain white copier paper

List of vocabulary words

Pencils

PREPARATION

Make up to five copies of the reproducible for each student, so the student has one sheet for each vocabulary word. We recommend that each student work with no more than five words during one lesson.

STEP BY STEP

☆ Each student, working independently, decides which words to put in his word diary.

☆ Using a separate copy of the reproducible for each vocabulary word, the student starts in the first section of the paper and writes the word in an unusual way. He might use bubble letters, broken-lined letters, dotted letters, block letters, etc.

☆ In the second section, the student writes on the webbed lines words that rhyme with the vocabulary word, or ones that have the same beginning or ending sound.

☆ In the third section, the student draws an illustration of the word or of something that would bring the word to mind for him. For example, for the word "strong," he might draw a set of barbells.

☆ In the last section of the page, the student writes one to four sentences (depending on grade level) using the new word.

VARIATIONS

For a whole-class activity, make a transparency of the reproducible, display it on the overhead projector, and incorporate all students' suggestions.

Write the diary entries and their associations on chart paper and post the list in the classroom.

Compile a class diary of difficult words and store it on the reference shelf with the classroom dictionaries.

GRADES: *1–6*
GROUP SIZE: *individual*

WHEN TO USE: *before reading*
FOCUS: *vocabulary recognition & association*

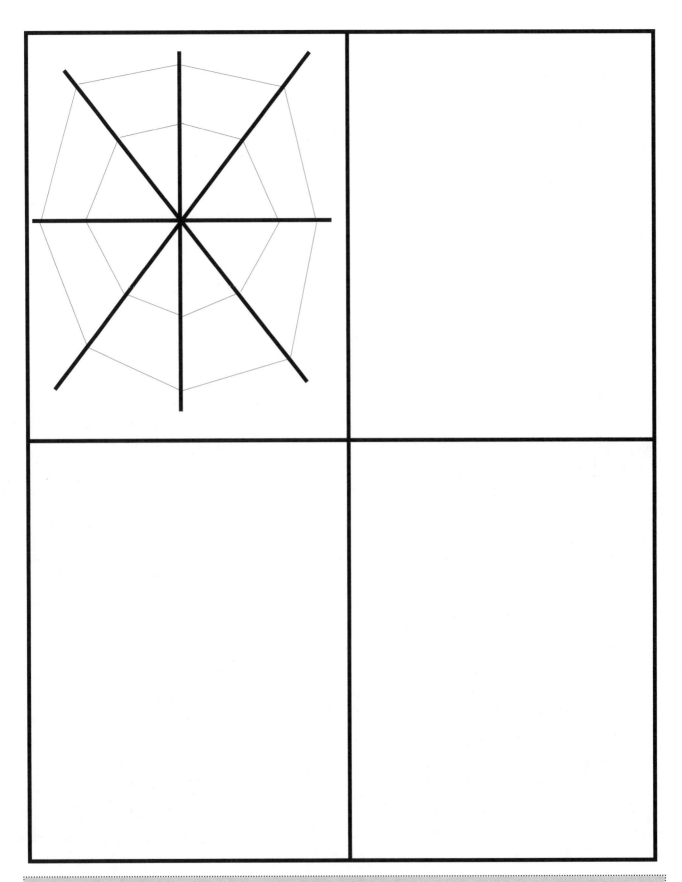

Boogie Bugs

Critter magnets add fun and movement to vocabulary study, as they "boogie" up and down a list of words.

MATERIALS

List of vocabulary words

3 refrigerator magnets

PREPARATION

Write the vocabulary words in a column on a magnetic chalkboard. Create two more columns and list the same words again in each column, each time in a different order.

STEP BY STEP

☆ Have one student stand in front of each column of words. Give each of the three students one of the magnets.

☆ Call out one of the words, and have each of the three students place his magnet (Boogie Bug) beside that word in his column.

☆ Repeat the process, with the same three students responding to the prompts and moving their magnets until all of the words have been called.

☆ With the same students at the board, begin the process again—but this time, instead of giving the word itself, give a *clue* to each word. You might give a synonym, an antonym, a word that rhymes with one of the vocabulary words, a word that begins or ends the same way, a context clue (a sentence with a blank for the word), or a definition.

☆ Have each student place his Boogie Bug next to the word suggested by the clue. For example, if you say, "Find a synonym for the word 'big,'" a student might place his Boogie Bug next to the word "large."

☆ Once again call out the words themselves, and instruct students to again move the Boogie Bugs next to those words. This time, though, the pace speeds up because this is the "lightning round." As you call out the words quickly and students move their Boogie Bugs, the magnets appear to "boogie" up and down the word list.

VARIATIONS

With kindergarten students, use letters, shapes, colors, names, or numerals in place of sight words.

With grades three through six, use words, dates, definitions, or names from content areas.

TEACHER TIP

Insect magnets are the perfect manipulative for this activity.

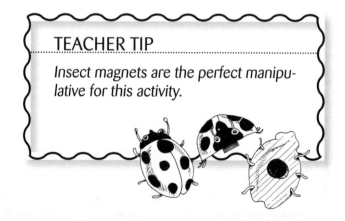

GRADES: *1–3*
GROUP SIZE: *3 students*

WHEN TO USE: *before & after reading*
FOCUS: *vocabulary recognition & association*

Fast Flashlight Focus

In this fast-paced, interactive activity for building vocabulary associations, adult-sized flashlights give new meaning to the word "focus."

MATERIALS

List of 10–15 vocabulary words

10–15 large index cards

Markers

Clothesline (optional)

Clothespins (optional)

7–8 inexpensive flashlights with batteries

Replacement batteries

PREPARATION

Write one vocabulary word on each card. Display the word cards on the wall, chalkboard tray, or bulletin board, or stretch a clothesline across the classroom and attach the cards to it with clothespins.

STEP BY STEP

☆ Students sit on the floor in three horizontal rows, with each student in the front row holding a flashlight. (Students in the second and third rows watch until it's their turn.)

☆ As you name each displayed vocabulary word, all of the students with flashlights focus their lights on the designated word.

☆ Repeat the process, but this time, instead of naming each word, give a clue to it (an antonym, a synonym, a rhyming word, etc.). The children with flashlights focus on the word suggested by the clue.

☆ Once again call out the words, but this time do it quickly. Students "fast focus" on each word as it's called.

☆ Rotate the rows of students, and let the students in the new first row repeat the process.

☆ Continue until all students have had a chance to participate in each of the three steps.

VARIATIONS

Explain the process during a parent meeting. Give a list of vocabulary words, along with a free flashlight, to each family. Encourage parents to help their students "fast focus" at home.

For kindergarten students, use letters, colors, numerals, shapes, or names of words.

TEACHER TIP

You can use this activity to assess student word-recognition and word-association skills quickly.

GRADES: *1–3*
GROUP SIZE: *whole group*

WHEN TO USE: *before & after reading*
FOCUS: *vocabulary recognition & association*

3-D Delight

The 3-D effect transforms an ordinary vocabulary list into something magical that captures student attention.

MATERIALS

Sunglasses reproducible (see page 27)

Card stock

Red cellophane

Green cellophane

Crayons

1 sheet of paper for each student

Glue

1 red marker for each student

1 green marker for each student

Scissors for each student

PREPARATION

Copy the reproducible onto card stock, making one copy for each student. Cut the cellophane into 2½" x 2" pieces, creating one red piece and one green piece for each student. Give each student a copy of the reproducible, along with one red and one green piece of cellophane.

STEP BY STEP

☆ Each student colors, then cuts out and folds the glasses pattern, being sure to cut openings for the "lenses."

☆ Each child glues a red piece of cellophane behind one of the lens openings and a green piece behind the other opening, then trims off any excess cellophane. These pieces of cellophane will serve as the lenses.

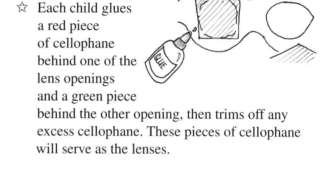

☆ Each student glues the sides to the front of his glasses.

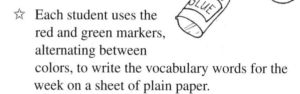

☆ Each student uses the red and green markers, alternating between colors, to write the vocabulary words for the week on a sheet of plain paper.

☆ Students read the words through their "sunglasses." Children typically are awed and delighted to see their words appear to become "3-D."

TEACHER TIP

Inexpensive cellophane can be found with the wrapping paper in most department stores. Or if you prefer, you can use colored acetate report covers.

GRADES: *K–3*
GROUP SIZE: *individual*

WHEN TO USE: *before & after reading*
FOCUS: *vocabulary recognition*

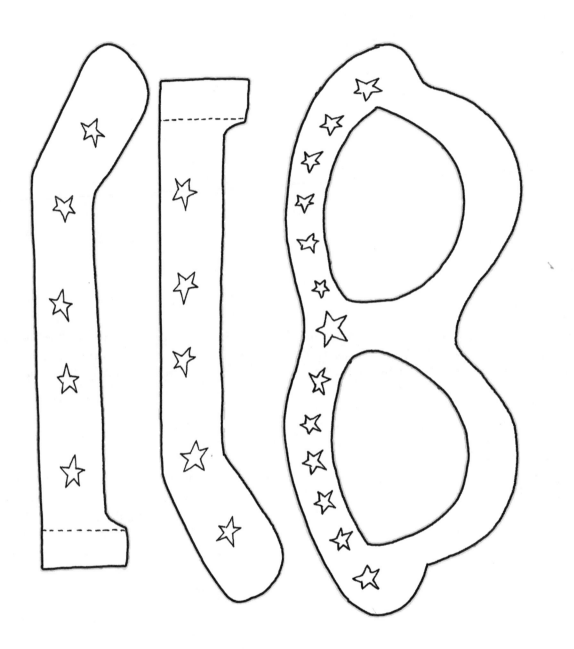

Partners on Parade

Students make connections, problem solve, and parade around the room with their words. Music makes this activity a favorite with kinesthetic learners.

MATERIALS

List of words to be practiced

1 large index card for each student

Marker

Hole punch

1 piece of yarn or string (20" long) for each card

Musical CD or tape and player

PREPARATION

The words to be practiced can be sight words, words from a particular story or unit, skill words, or any combination of these. You'll need one word for every two students—so if there are twenty students in the class, you'll need ten words. Write each of the practice words on a separate index card. Write an associative word for each practice word on one of the remaining index cards (one association per card). Use synonyms, antonyms, contractions, definitions, word families, like endings, like beginnings, etc. Punch two holes in each card and attach the yarn or string to make a "word bib" for each child. This leaves students' hands free.

STEP BY STEP

☆ Give each student a prepared word bib to hang around her neck.

☆ Start the music, then call out a practice word.

☆ The student wearing that word proceeds to march around the room.

☆ Continue calling out practice words and having students join the parade until half of the class is marching.

☆ One at a time, call on each of the remaining students by name to make an association and join his partner. For example, a student whose bib has the antonym "day" or the rhyming word "sight" might join the child with the practice word "night."

☆ Have all the partners march around the room together in a parade of words.

☆ Follow up with a discussion of how the words were related. Allow each child to explain the strategy he used to make an association for his word.

TEACHER TIP

Since this activity is based on the student's opinion and personal association, accept all answers. As long as the child can justify his answer, it's correct.

VARIATIONS

For an individual activity or a small-group center, place a magnet on the back of each card. Students can match the pairs on a magnetic board.

To review and associate content material, substitute words and concepts from the content areas.

Substitute math vocabulary and concepts to reinforce understanding of those terms.

GRADES: *K–3*
GROUP SIZE: *whole group*

WHEN TO USE: *before & after reading*
FOCUS: *vocabulary review & association*

Gimme a Break!

Students try to bluff their classmates as they build vocabulary retention skills in this lively, fast-moving game.

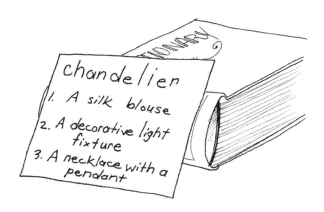

MATERIALS

List of vocabulary words or spelling words

1 index card for each word

Marker

1 dictionary for each student

Pencils

1 clicker for each team

PREPARATION

Write one vocabulary word at the top of each card. Hand one card to each student. Divide the class into two teams.

STEP BY STEP

☆ Using the dictionary and her imagination, each child writes on her card two false definitions for her word, plus the correct definition. She numbers the definitions 1, 2, and 3, but does not necessarily use Number 1 for the correct answer.

☆ The first student on Team A reads all three of her definitions aloud. Then she chooses one to read again, telling the other team that this is the correct definition. This may truly be the correct definition, or the student may be bluffing.

☆ Now Team B has a chance to respond. If a member of Team B thinks the definition that was just read is correct, she sounds the clicker. If she thinks it was a bluff, she says, "Gimme a Break!" and states what she believes to be the real definition. If her response is correct, she wins a point for her team.

☆ Play goes to Team B. The first player on that team reads all of the definitions on his card, choosing one to read again, and the process is repeated.

☆ Play continues, alternating between teams, until all word cards have been used.

☆ The team with the most points wins.

FOR EXAMPLE

Model for students how to write the definitions, so they see that the made-up definitions should be believable and the correct answer should not always be Number 1.

VARIATIONS

In place of clickers, use bells or anything else that makes a noise.

Use this activity with content words to maximize comprehension and retention of content definitions.

GRADES: *2–6*
GROUP SIZE: *whole group*

WHEN TO USE: *before or after reading*
FOCUS: *vocabulary retention*

Red Light, Green Light

Here's the perfect word-study activity for the child who has a short attention span, the child who learns best while moving, and that special child who just can't seem to sit still for even a short time.

MATERIALS

List of 20–30 vocabulary words

20–30 small index cards

Markers

PREPARATION

Write one vocabulary word on each index card. Place the cards word side up around the edge of a table or in a circle on the floor.

STEP BY STEP

☆ Students form a circle around the table or around the words on the floor.

☆ When you say "green light," the students walk around the table in a clockwise direction.

☆ When you say "red light," the students stop.

☆ One at a time, going around the circle, each student names the word on the card in front of him and then turns the card face down.

☆ You replace each turned-over card with a face-up card that has a new word on it, then say "green light" again.

☆ Students repeat the process.

> ### TEACHER TIP
>
> *For more fun and listening practice, add "reverse" to the directions, so students can walk backward before you give the "red light" command.*

VARIATIONS

For mental math practice, write equations on the cards and have students solve them.

Share this activity with parents as an enjoyable and easy way to practice words at home.

After the student names his word, have him use it in a sentence.

GRADES: *K–3*   **WHEN TO USE:** *before & after reading*
GROUP SIZE: *8–10 students*   **FOCUS:** *vocabulary recognition*

You've Got Mail

This activity develops teamwork and precision—and builds fluent sight-word readers, too.

MATERIALS

Approximately 2 vocabulary words per student

1 index card per vocabulary word

Marker

PREPARATION

Write one vocabulary word on each index card.

STEP BY STEP

☆ Have students sit in a circle on the floor.

☆ Hand one word card to each student. Place extra word cards in the center of the circle to be exchanged if needed.

☆ Begin the activity by saying, "Circulate the mail." This means that each student is to pass his card, word side up, to the person on his left. At the same time, he's to use his other hand to accept another card from the person on his right.

☆ Students keep passing cards until you say, "You've got mail."

☆ At that point, go around the circle, asking each student in turn to read the word he's holding.

☆ Repeat four or five times. (After the first two or three rounds, you may want to have some or all students exchange their cards for new ones from the center of the circle.)

VARIATIONS

Rather than asking them just to name the words, require each student to use the word in a sentence or give its definition.

Practice math facts by writing problems on the cards. When they "get mail," students solve the problems.

Practice phonics by writing word families on the cards and asking each student to give an appropriate example for the word family on his card. For example, if you write the word family "-am" on the card, the student could respond with "ham," "slam," or "clam."

GRADES: *K–3*
GROUP SIZE: *8–12 students*

WHEN TO USE: *before or after reading*
FOCUS: *vocabulary*

Bright Idea

As students make personal associations, they gain ownership of vocabulary words.

MATERIALS

List of 6 vocabulary words

6 sheets of 18" X 12" construction paper

Marker

Lightbulb reproducible (see page 33)

Plain white copier paper

PREPARATION

Write one vocabulary word on each piece of construction paper and hang the sheets of paper in different places around the classroom. Make one copy of the reproducible for every two students. On each lightbulb, write one association for one of the vocabulary words (be sure to create three to four lightbulbs to go with each vocabulary word). Associations can include synonyms, antonyms, rhyming words, illustrations, definitions, word configurations, word families, and sentences with blanks. Each association can be a word, a phrase, or an illustration.

STEP BY STEP

☆ Give each student a prepared lightbulb.

☆ Explain that when you say "Make an association!" every student in the class is to simultaneously move to a wall word (on the construction paper) that has an association with her lightbulb.

☆ Give students time to make their associations. Since these are personal associations, it's possible that a student will be able to make more than one association for his word. However, the student must choose only one wall word.

☆ When all students are standing beside their choices, have them take turns explaining the "bright idea" strategies they used in making their associations. Every answer is acceptable because all answers are based on personal associations.

VARIATIONS

Have students write their own associations on the lightbulbs.

For content-area study, write appropriate science, health, or social-studies vocabulary words on the sheets of construction paper.

Use math facts or math vocabulary. For example, you might write "6 + 8 = ?" on one of the pieces of construction paper, and create lightbulbs that include an illustration of fourteen apples, "10 + 4," and the word "fourteen."

GRADES: *K–3*
GROUP SIZE: *whole group*

WHEN TO USE: *after reading*
FOCUS: *vocabulary recognition & association*

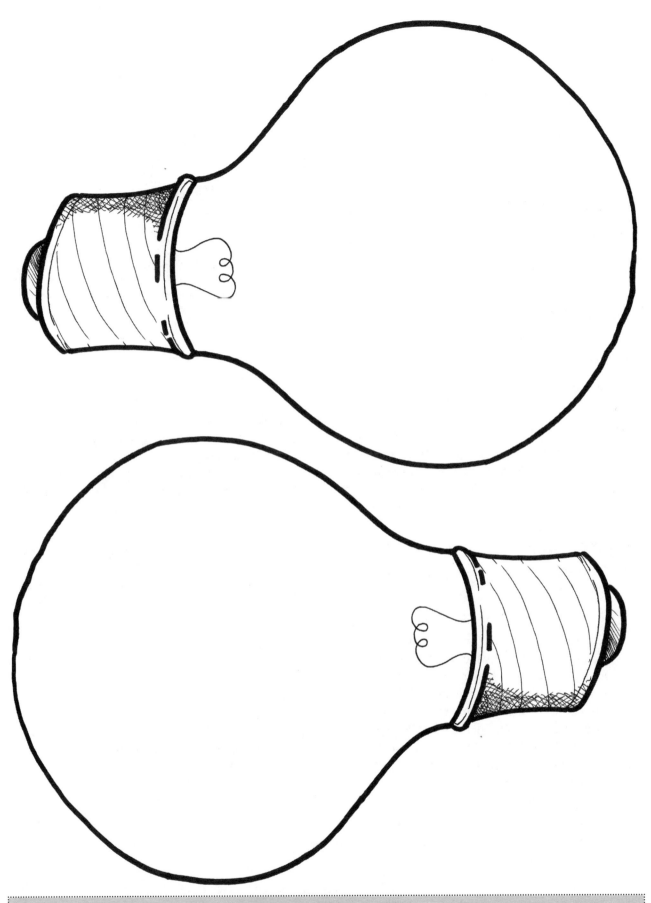

SODA Hunt

This activity provides a fun purpose for finding context clues. Once students have plenty of practice with SODA, it can become a strategy they automatically fall back on to determine word meanings.

MATERIALS

Bookmark reproducible (see page 35)

Card stock

Markers or crayons

PREPARATION

Make enough copies of the reproducible so that each child can have one bookmark. Cut the bookmarks apart and give one to each student, along with markers or crayons.

STEP BY STEP

☆ Have each child trace the word SODA on her bookmark.

☆ Instruct students to color their bookmarks.

☆ Use real text to model for students how to complete a SODA hunt by looking for context clues. Explain that if they keep reading, they're likely to find at least one of the elements of SODA: a word that means the <u>s</u>ame thing, a word that means the <u>o</u>pposite, a <u>d</u>efinition (although it may not always be right next to the word in question), or <u>a</u>nything else (a picture, a graph, the way the word is used, etc.).

☆ Tell students that each child should keep his SODA bookmark in the book he's reading as a constant reminder to use the strategy.

☆ Explain that when a student comes to a word he doesn't know, he should continue reading to the end of the paragraph or page (to avoid disrupting concentration and comprehension), then go on a SODA hunt, searching for the elements of SODA.

☆ Follow up by consistently reminding students to go on SODA hunts when they come to words they don't know. For example, in *Piggins*, Jane Yolen refers to a missing lavalier. Students must continue reading to the end of the page to determine that a lavalier is a necklace.

VARIATION

For older students, the SODA strategy can evolve into the SAID strategy. In this case the <u>s</u> is for synonym, <u>a</u> is for antonym, <u>i</u> is for interesting facts, and <u>d</u> is for definition.

GRADES: *1–6*

GROUP SIZE: *individual*

WHEN TO USE: *during reading*

FOCUS: *vocabulary comprehension & context clues*

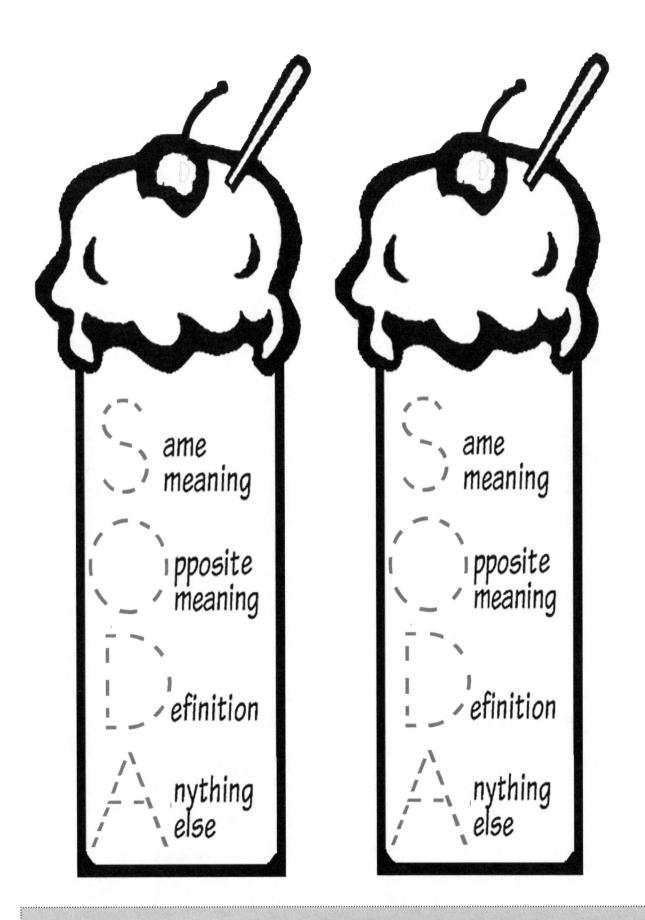

S ame meaning

O pposite meaning

D efinition

A nything else

Lit Logs

A Lit Log can take the form of a spiral notebook or a small notepad that's used over the long term. But these individual logs, constructed from scratch for each story, are more personal and more fun. Regular use of this response journal helps students to become more conscientious learners and transfers the responsibility for learning from the teacher to the student.

MATERIALS

2 sheets of 8½" X 11" paper for each student

Pencils

Scissors

PREPARATION

Give two sheets of paper to each student.

STEP BY STEP

The actual construction of a Lit Log is a lesson in listening and following directions. The directions to students go like this:

☆ Put two sheets together and fold them in half. (The goal is to end up with a "hamburger fold," not a "hot-dog fold.") Separate the sheets, but keep each sheet folded.

☆ On Sheet 1, place two dots on the fold, one approximately one to two inches in from each end. Draw a line connecting the two dots, keeping the pencil about ⅛" from the fold.

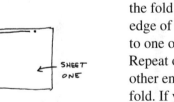

☆ Cut along that line so that when the sheet is opened, you have a long thin window.

☆ Refold Sheet 1 and lay it on top of the folded Sheet 2 so that the folds are aligned. Place a dot on Sheet 2 to mark where you started cutting Sheet 1 and another to mark where you stopped. Lay Sheet 1 aside.

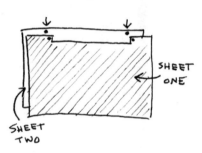

☆ Open Sheet 2 and cut a slit on the fold from the edge of the paper to one of the dots. Repeat on the other end of the fold. If you need more pages, add more sheets and cut the slits identically.

GRADES: *2–6*   **WHEN TO USE:** *before, during & after reading*

GROUP SIZE: *individual*   **FOCUS:** *comprehension*

☆ Starting from the long side, loosely fold Sheet 2 so that the slits are on top of each other.

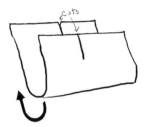

☆ Open Sheet 1. Insert the folded Sheet 2 half way through the window of Sheet 1.

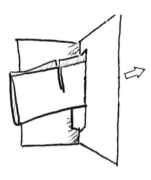

☆ Unfold Sheet 2 to form a book. Decorate the cover of your Lit Log. Keep your Lit Log beside you during reading class.

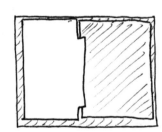

Once the students have made their Lit Logs, stop at any point during a reading lesson to pose a question and give students time to respond in their logs. You may also want to display the completed logs in the classroom.

VARIATIONS

Use completed Lit Logs for assessment.

Include completed Lit Logs in student portfoios and/or in parent conferences.

Story Sacks

An ordinary paper lunch bag becomes a "story sack," holding vocabulary clues that remind students of the key elements in a story.

MATERIALS

1 story for each group

10 index cards per group

1 brown or white lunch sack for each group

Markers or crayons

PREPARATION

Divide the class into groups and have each group read a different story. Hand out the index cards, lunch sacks, and markers or crayons.

STEP BY STEP

☆ Tell the class that each group is to scan its book and find up to ten key words, in sequence, that will help them retell the story. You may want to give an example—perhaps explaining that key words for *Goldilocks and the Three Bears* might be "family," "porridge," "forest," "Goldilocks," "hot," "chair," "bed," etc.

☆ Have students write each key word on a card, then add an illustration of the word.

☆ Ask each group to put their completed cards in order, number the cards sequentially, and place them in the sack.

☆ When everyone's ready, have the students in each group remove the cards from the bag, place them in the correct sequence, and then take turns retelling the story to the rest of the class as they pick up the cards in order.

☆ Ask each group to illustrate its sack with a picture that pertains to the story.

☆ If you like, display sacks and cards on a bulletin board or place them in a center where other students can use them to practice sequencing or retelling the story.

VARIATIONS

To encourage parental involvement, use this as a home activity. In this case, instruct students to place actual items or pictures of items, rather than words, in the sack to aid in retelling. Explain that they should bring the sacks back to school to share with the class.

When working with content text that has a logical sequence to it (for example, text about the life cycle of a butterfly), use vocabulary words as key words.

For kindergarten students, we've found it's helpful to provide the key words and have students illustrate the cards.

GRADES: *K–6*
GROUP SIZE: *2–3 students*

WHEN TO USE: *after reading*
FOCUS: *comprehension, sequencing & retelling*

Story Sandwich

When studying the elements of a story that includes sequencing, it's useful for students to have a guide that helps them determine the integral parts and the sequence of events. In this activity, the order and ingredients of a sandwich help students remember the order and ingredients of a story.

MATERIALS

Reproducibles for sandwich pieces (see pages 40–41)

Card stock

Pencils

1 large-head brass fastener per child

PREPARATION

Copy the reproducibles onto card stock, making enough copies so that each child can have a full set of five pieces. (You will need to make two copies of the bread reproducible for each student.)

STEP BY STEP

☆ Hand out the brass fasteners and the copies of the reproducibles.

☆ As you write on the board the basic parts of a story, have the students copy each label onto the appropriate sandwich piece. Model how they can use each of the sandwich pieces to help them remember a specific element of the story. We suggest labeling the pieces like this:

Top piece of bread: lead or topic sentence

Lettuce: the setting and the main character(s)

Cheese: a problem or situation that occurs in the story

Lunch meat: what results from the problem or situation

Bottom piece of bread: solution or ending to the story

☆ Explain that each student should place his sandwich pieces in order and use a brass fastener to hold the pieces together.

☆ Each student now has a guideline to help him identify the elements and sequence of a story as he reads.

VARIATIONS

When you're reading a story to the students, use the story sandwich to point out the parts of the story and the order in which they appear.

Have students refer to their "sandwiches" as guides for their own writing, reinforcing sequencing.

GRADES: *1–6*
GROUP SIZE: *individual*

WHEN TO USE: *before, during & after reading*
FOCUS: *reading comprehension, sequencing & identifying story elements*

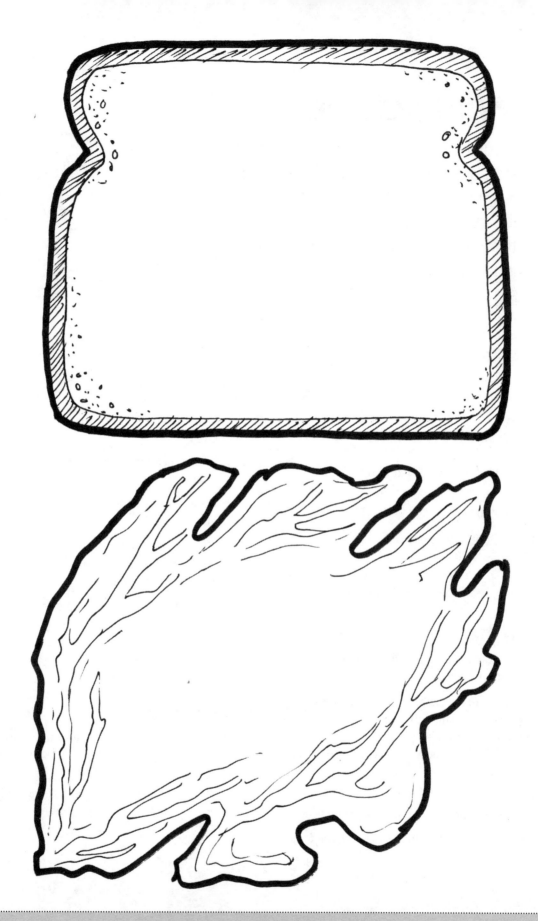

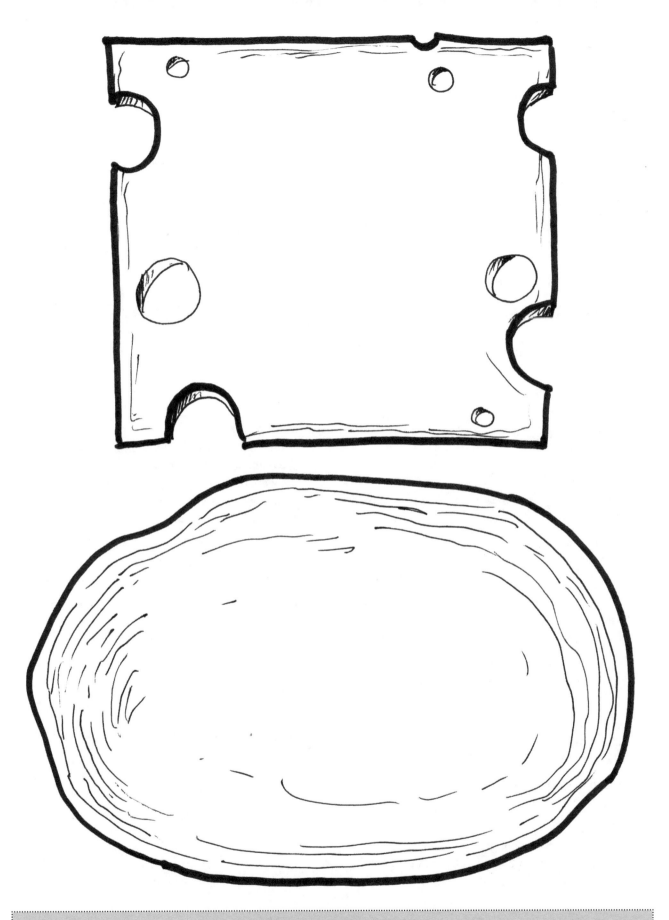

Ask, Ask Away!

By learning to ask questions and answer them as they read, students improve their reading comprehension. This activity works especially well in guided reading groups.

Who **What** **Why** **Where** **When** **How**

MATERIALS

Cards reproducible (see page 43)

1 story

PREPARATION

Using card stock, make two copies of the reproducible. Cut the cards apart.

STEP BY STEP

☆ Tell students to use the six question words to create questions in their heads as they read.

☆ Have each student read the story of the day on her own.

☆ Divide the students into an even number of teams, each team containing approximately six students. For this example, let's say you're working with two teams of six students each.

☆ Give each member of Team A one card with a question word. Distribute the second set of question cards to the members of Team B.

☆ Have each student on Team A create a question about the story. Each question must begin with the word on that student's index card.

☆ Ask one of the students from Team A to read her question aloud and choose a member of Team B to answer it.

☆ If the Team B student gives the correct answer, his team scores a point and he poses the next question, following the same procedure.

☆ If the Team B student gives an incorrect answer, the team does not score a point. You ask for other answers until someone volunteers the correct response. Then you choose someone from Team B to ask the next question.

☆ Continue in this way until all students have had a chance to ask questions. Then have students shuffle the cards and repeat the process.

☆ Continue the game until no more questions can be formed.

VARIATIONS

Give each student a question card *before* he reads the story, so he can use the word on the card to form questions as he reads.

Use this as an individual activity, having students write and answer their own questions.

GRADES: *3–6*
GROUP SIZE: *at least 2 teams of 6 students each*

WHEN TO USE: *during & after reading*
FOCUS: *comprehension development through questioning*

Who

What

Where

Why

When

How

Predict/React Journal

Through this simple journal students learn the strategy of predicting while reading. They also learn to revisit their predictions and revise them if needed.

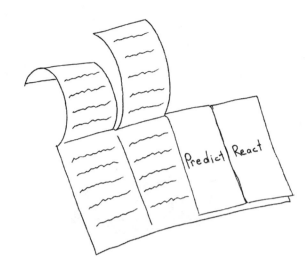

MATERIALS

1 story

1 sheet of paper per child (size depends on the level of the student)

Scissors

PREPARATION

Read the story ahead of time and identify the point—just before the climax—at which you want students to stop reading and revise their predictions.

STEP BY STEP

☆ Give each child a sheet of paper.

☆ The goal is for each child to make a flip book with four flip doors to open. To start the flip book, have each child fold the paper in half vertically.

☆ Next, the student should unfold the paper and make three evenly spaced cuts. Each cut should go from the long edge of the paper just to the fold.

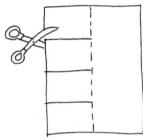

☆ Ask the student to re-fold the sheet so that the flip doors are facing him.

☆ On the first flip door, have the student write the word "predict"; on the second, "react"; on the third, "predict"; and on the fourth, "react."

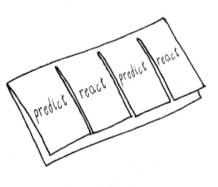

☆ Tell the class that this activity will help them to predict or guess what's going to happen in a story and then, after they read more, will give them a chance to react to their earlier predictions.

GRADES: *1–6*
GROUP SIZE: *individual*

WHEN TO USE: *before, during & after reading*
FOCUS: *making, revising & confirming predictions*

☆ Explain that each student should look at the front of the book, especially the title, then lift the first "predict" flap of her flip book and predict in writing what she thinks the story is going to be about.

☆ Have each student read the story independently, up to the place you've identified as the stopping point.

☆ Ask each student to lift the second door of his flip book and write his reaction to his earlier prediction(s) now that he has more information from the story itself. For example, a student who predicted that Cinderella was about a poor, mistreated girl might say, "Wow, I was right about the main character, but I didn't think there would be fantasy characters in the story."

☆ Have the class discuss their initial predictions and their reactions.

☆ Explain that now each student should make a final prediction as to what he thinks will happen in the story and write that prediction under the third door of the flip book.

☆ Have students share their new predictions with one another.

☆ Instruct students to read to the end of the story, again working independently.

☆ Ask each student to write a reaction to her final predictions under the last door.

☆ Follow up with a class discussion about the second set of predictions and reactions.

VARIATIONS

Following each prediction and reaction, have students place their flip books on their desks and then walk from one desk to another, reading one another's predictions and reactions. This gives the students an opportunity to showcase their writing as well as to compare their classmates' predictions and reactions with their own.

When working with chapter books, you may want to have each student create more than one Predict/React Journal per book.

Memory Boosters

Get students moving and making connections as they catch the ball and name the facts they've memorized. Use this activity at the culmination of a content unit, prior to formal evaluation, to boost comprehension and help students retain factual information.

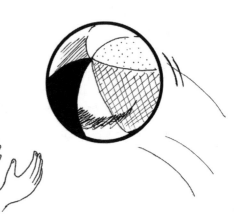

MATERIALS
1 small index card per fact

Marker

1 large beach ball (or any soft ball)

PREPARATION
Write on each index card a content fact for the unit the class is studying or has just completed. For example, after the class completes a unit on penguins, you might write on one card, "The mother penguin recognizes the father penguin by his voice." On another, you might put, "The father penguin carries the egg on his feet to keep it warm." Create one card for every fact you would like students to know.

STEP BY STEP
☆ Give each child one fact card and tell the child that he is going to become an expert on that fact. Explain that he should take the card home with him at the end of the day, repeat the fact over and over, and memorize it.

☆ Memorize one fact yourself.

☆ The next day, have half the class (approximately ten to thirteen students) stand in a circle. To maximize listening, ask the other students to sit inside the circle at the feet of the standing students. Everyone should face the center of the circle.

☆ While holding the beach ball, state the fact you memorized and ask students to repeat it.

☆ Do this several times.

☆ Toss the beach ball to a student. Let's say that student is Joe. Ask Joe to state his fact.

☆ Direct the class to repeat that fact.

☆ Follow the state-and-repeat process several times for the same fact.

☆ Have Joe toss the ball to another student. Let's say that student is Adam.

☆ Instruct Adam to state his fact; have the class repeat it.

☆ Ask Adam to make a connection between his and any other fact that another student has given. (This does not have to be the student who had the ball last.) For example, if Adam stated that an emperor penguin dad carries the egg on his feet, he might find a connection with a student who said that the dad emperor penguins huddle together during extremely cold weather.

☆ Have Adam toss the ball to another student. Repeat the process.

☆ Continue tossing the ball, stating and repeating facts, and making connections until every student has had a turn with the beach ball.

☆ Have the seated students change places with those who are standing. Then start all over again!

GRADES: *2–6*
GROUP SIZE: *whole group*

WHEN TO USE: *after reading*
FOCUS: *comprehension*

Frame a Story

As students create simple drawings about a story, they learn what to look for in the story and become more engaged with their reading.

MATERIALS

1 four-foot section of butcher paper per group

Crayons or markers

Any trade book (1 copy for each student)

PREPARATION

Take the butcher paper and fold it in thirds. At the top of the first section, write the word "Setting." At the top of the second section, write the words "Main Characters." At the top of the third section, write the words "What Happens." Divide the students into groups of three or four. Give each student a copy of the trade book to be read.

STEP BY STEP

☆ Have the students look at the front cover of the book and discuss within their groups what they think the story might be about.

☆ Tell the students the names of the main characters and one fact about each main character. For example, in the story *The Tortoise and the Hare*, you might tell the students that the two main characters are the tortoise, who's very slow, and the hare, who's very fast.

☆ Give each group a sheet of butcher paper.

☆ Ask the students to draw pictures in the first section of the butcher paper to show what they think the setting might be, in the second section to show what they think the characters might look like, and in the third section to show what they think might happen in the story. (It's help-

ful to caution students not to write on the backs of their papers if they don't like their first drawings. They'll need that space later.)

☆ Post the drawings in the classroom.

☆ Read the story aloud to the students as they follow along silently.

☆ Give the students time to discuss what they thought about the three main elements of the story. Ask how the drawings of their predictions are different from the actual setting, characters, and plot.

☆ Have each group return to their original drawings and create new drawings on the back of each sheet of butcher paper. The new drawings should reflect what they've learned about each of the three elements from reading the story. Be sure to encourage them to add detail.

VARIATIONS

Have one group draw the three elements on the front of their sheet and another group, after following along as the teacher reads the story, re-create the elements on the back.

Ask students to draw their own comic-strip frames for this activity and work within those frames.

GRADES: *2–6*
GROUP SIZE: *3–4 students*

WHEN TO USE: *before, during & after reading*
FOCUS: *comprehension & story elements*

Just Because

This easy-to-make flip book demon-strates in a very visual way the relation-ship between cause and effect.

MATERIALS

1 sheet of white drawing paper (12" X 18") for each student

Scissors

Crayons

STEP BY STEP

☆ Ask each student to make a flip book by folding his paper in half lengthwise and cutting the top layer in three places from the edge to the fold. Show students how to make one cut to divide that top layer in half, then two more cuts to divide it into fourths. Students should be careful not to cut through both halves of the paper. The paper will now appear to have four doors, each of which will flip up to reveal what's underneath.

FOR EXAMPLE

Causes you might want to consider for this activity include:

It's my birthday

It's storming outside

I overslept

I studied my spelling words

It snowed all night

You and your students are sure to come up with many more!

☆ Brainstorm with the class to generate some causes.

☆ Ask each student to write one cause on the top of each flip door.

☆ Have the student lift each flip door and under-neath write a corresponding effect for each cause, so that when the student opens the door, he sees the effect.

☆ Ask students to illustrate and color the effects they've described in words.

☆ Have the class discuss and share their flip books.

VARIATIONS

Choose only one cause. Have each student write the same cause across all four doors, then name four different effects, writing one under each flip door. Finally, have students illustrate and color their work.

Instruct each student to cut four pictures from magazines, glue one on each flip door, and write under each door the effects of what happened in that picture.

Ask each child to write one cause on each of the four doors of the flip book, then exchange books with a partner. The partner should then write one effect under each flip door.

GRADES: *1–3*
GROUP SIZE: *individual*

WHEN TO USE: *during skills groups*
FOCUS: *cause & effect*

Shirt Tales

Use this quick-and-easy shirt book to help students understand character development and analysis.

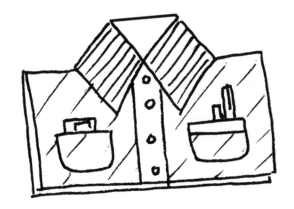

MATERIALS

1 trade book

1 sheet of paper (any size) for each student

Scissors

Glue

Jewelry, ribbons, sequins, and other decorations

Pencils

STEP BY STEP

☆ The class reads a book that includes at least one strong character.

☆ Each student chooses a character from the book to focus on.

☆ The booklet for this activity looks like a shirt. To begin the shirt, each student folds a sheet of paper in half horizontally. Then he makes two cuts, each two inches long, near the fold, cutting through both layers from each edge toward the center. Each cut should be placed two inches down from the fold and parallel to it.

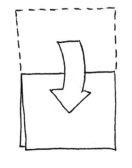

☆ Each student folds down the two cut sections until they meet in the center of the paper, forming a shirt collar. The student glues the bottom portions of the collar to the paper.

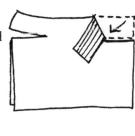

☆ Students decorate their shirts with pockets, jewelry, ribbons, sequins, or anything else that's appropriate for the characters they've chosen.

☆ Once the shirts are made and decorated, students form groups by character. (All those who chose Goldilocks meet in one group; all those who chose Baby Bear are in a different group.)

☆ Each student develops a character analysis using information from the story. On the paper underneath the decorated shirt front, the student writes a description of the character she's chosen and tells about that character's thoughts and actions in the story. Group members help each other by discussing their characters.

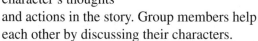

☆ Each student introduces her character to the class.

GRADES: *1–6*
GROUP SIZE: *individual, with small-group component*

WHEN TO USE: *after reading*
FOCUS: *character analysis*

Have a Ball with Questions

When students create questions, they learn the art of questioning and at the same time build comprehension.

MATERIALS

1 permanent marker

1 inflatable beach ball (available from discount or online novelty stores)

1 story

PREPARATION

Using the permanent marker, write one of the six question words ("who," "what," "when," "where," "how," "why") on each colored section of the beach ball. This becomes the Question Ball.

STEP BY STEP

☆ Have students read a story together as a class or in small guided-reading groups, then discuss the story together.

☆ Follow the discussion by introducing the Question Ball. Explain that you're going to toss it to a student, who should catch it with both hands.

☆ When the student catches the ball, the question word that's closest to his right index finger is his word for this turn. He must use that word to ask a question about the story. For example, if the book is *The True Story of the Three Little Pigs*, by Jon Scieszka, and the student has the word "what," he might ask, "What illness did the wolf have in the story?"

☆ Call on another student in the group to answer the question.

VARIATION

Instead of a question ball, create a question box. Seal or fold the top closed, then write one question word on each side of the box. Instruct students to roll the box as they'd roll a die in a game of chance. The word that's on top becomes the student's question word.

TEACHER TIP

As the game continues, encourage students to move from literal to higher-level questions.

GRADES: *2–6*
GROUP SIZE: *small group or whole class*

WHEN TO USE: *after reading*
FOCUS: *comprehension through questioning*

Mask a Character

Invite students to "become" the characters in their books and you'll help them create lifelong connections.

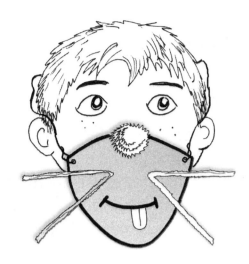

MATERIALS

1 painter's mask for each student

Markers

Pipe cleaners, yarn, and other craft items

Sunglasses, wigs, earrings, and other accessories

STEP BY STEP

☆ Each student chooses his favorite character from a book the class has been reading.

☆ Using the materials provided, he creates on his painter's mask the facial features of the character, adding embellishments as he chooses. Pipe cleaners make good whiskers, yarn can become a mustache, etc.

☆ Each child dons his decorated mask. As he does this, he "becomes" his character.

☆ Students ask each other questions about the characters and the stories. For example, someone talking to the mouse from *If You Give a Mouse a Cookie* might ask him why he likes cookies.

☆ Each student responds as the character represented by his mask.

TEACHER TIP

A painter's mask (also called a "dust mask") is shaped something like a snout and has an elastic band to hold it on a student's head. Look for these masks in hardware stores.

VARIATION

Have three to four students don their masks and work together to create a new story featuring their characters.

GRADES: *1–3*
GROUP SIZE: *large or small group with students working individually*

WHEN TO USE: *during & after reading*
FOCUS: *comprehension*

The Main-Idea Hand

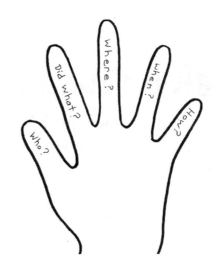

Students often have difficulty identifying the central theme of a fictional story. With this strategy, students of any age can use the fingers on one hand to determine the main idea of a story.

MATERIALS

1 sheet of drawing paper for each student

Markers

STEP BY STEP

☆ Have each student trace his hand on his drawing paper.

☆ Ask each student to write the question words or phrases on the digits of the tracing as follows:

Thumb: Who?

Pointer: Did what?

Middle: Where?

Ring: When?

Pinky: How?

☆ Explain how the answers to these five questions combine to tell the main idea of the story.

☆ Collect the papers. Laminate each hand, then return the hand tracings to students. Remind them often to refer to these Main-Idea Hands any time they read (or listen to) a story. Repeating the question words and answering each one will tell them the main idea.

FOR EXAMPLE

If he's reading the story Cinderella and using the Main-Idea Hand to help him determine the main idea, a student's thought process might go something like this:

Who? Cinderella

Did what? Found a handsome prince

Where? At the ball

When? Before midnight

How? Because of her Fairy Godmother's spell

The main idea is that Cinderella met a handsome prince at the ball before midnight because of her Fairy Godmother's spell.

VARIATION

Have students compare answers to determine if the main idea can vary slightly.

GRADES: *2–6* **WHEN TO USE:** *during & after reading*
GROUP SIZE: *individual* **FOCUS:** *comprehension & identifying the main idea*

Compound Cut-Up Choo Choo

Students get creative with both drawings and words—nonsense and otherwise—that help them find the meanings of compound words.

MATERIALS

Reproducibles for train engine and caboose (see pages 54–55)

Plain white copier paper

Glue

2 shoe boxes

2 small index cards for each compound word

List of compound words

Drawing paper

Crayons or markers

PREPARATION

Make two copies of each of the reproducibles. Glue an engine to one of the shoe boxes and a caboose to the other. On each index card, write one part of a compound word from your list. For example, write "rain" on one card and "bow" on another. Place in the shoe-box engine all of the first parts of the compound words. All the remaining words go into the shoe-box caboose.

STEP BY STEP

☆ Have each student randomly choose one card from the engine and one card from the caboose to create a new compound word.

☆ Ask the student to write the new word, create a definition for it, and draw and color it.

☆ Display the compound-word drawings on a wall of the classroom. Place your second paper engine at the beginning and the second paper caboose at the end, and use the drawings as the train cars.

VARIATIONS

Use this activity to reinforce root words, prefixes, and suffixes.

Instead of drawing the new concepts, have students make 3-D models of their words out of clay or playdough.

FOR EXAMPLE

A student might choose "rain" as the first part of the new word and "ball" as the second part to create the word "rainball." For a definition, he might write, "a ball that bleeds raindrops." He might draw a ball that appears to be creating raindrops.

GRADES: *K–6*
GROUP SIZE: *individual*

WHEN TO USE: *during skills groups*
FOCUS: *working with words*

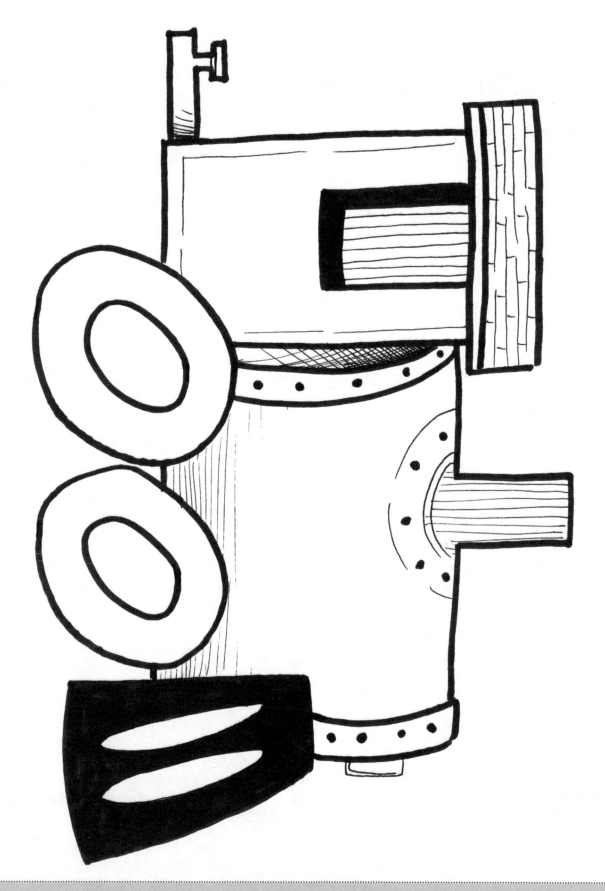

Luscious Lollipops

Students enjoy writing on balloons to describe themselves while learning the value of using adjectives and descriptive language.

MATERIALS

1 large half-sphere of Styrofoam

1 large gift box (roughly 12" X 12" X 12")

Glue

1 small bag of colored sand or pebbles

1 copy of the book *Luscious Lollipops*

1 large latex balloon for each student

1 permanent marker for each student

1 plastic balloon holder for each student (available online through novelty companies)

1 unbendable straw for each student

PREPARATION

Glue the flat side of the Styrofoam to the base of the gift box to display the finished "lollipops." Add the colored sand or pebbles to weigh down the box. Unless your students can handle the balloons on their own or by helping each other, blow up each balloon to the size of a soccer ball, and tie it closed.

STEP BY STEP

☆ Read the book *Luscious Lollipops,* by Ruth Heller, to the students. Be sure to point out the illustrations, as well as the adjectives that describe the nouns.

☆ Give every student an inflated balloon.

☆ Instruct each student to write his name on the top of the balloon with the permanent marker.

☆ On the rest of the balloon, ask him to write all the words or phrases he can think of to describe himself. Model the process with your own balloon. You might use words like "reader," "hiker," "love to cook," etc. to describe yourself.

☆ Give students a few examples to get them started. You might suggest words like "short," "happy," "bike rider," "blonde," etc.

GRADES: *1–6*
GROUP SIZE: *individual*

WHEN TO USE: *after reading*
FOCUS: *working with words*

☆ Discuss with the students the adjectives they chose, noting that these are describing words and that they make writing and speaking more interesting and polished.

☆ Have each student attach his balloon to a holder and insert a straw in the bottom of the holder. If necessary, add a drop of glue to secure the straw in the holder. (You may need to give students a hand with the balloon holder.) Each balloon becomes a student's "luscious lollipop."

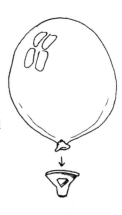

☆ Have students insert their lollipops into the Styrofoam in the gift box, creating a bouquet of lollipops for display.

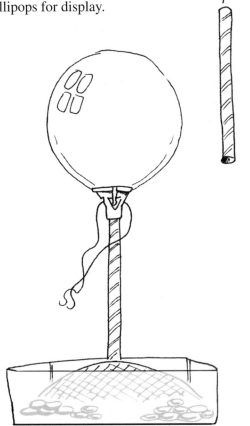

VARIATIONS

Ask each student to write someone else's name on the balloon and describe that person. It's fun to give the bouquets to nursing-home buddies or to another class of students whose names are on the balloons.

For a colorful bulletin board, follow the same process but substitute paper balloons and use yarn for balloon strings.

Keep materials together for a fun learning-center activity. Be sure to include instructions and a sample balloon!

Short Vowel Circle Sort

Young learners practice phonemic awareness as they sort real items in this interactive classroom game.

MATERIALS

Approximately 30 small items with short vowel sounds in their names

1 hat

1 net

1 dish

1 pot

1 child's umbrella (opened and turned upside down)

1 box to hold all items

PREPARATION

Collect the small items and place them inside the box.

STEP BY STEP

☆ Have students sit in a circle with the box of items in the center. Empty the box onto the floor and tell students the name of each item.

☆ Ask each student to select one item, name it, and tell which short vowel sound she hears in the word.

☆ Have the student place the item in the appropriate container for that vowel. Short "a" items go in the hat, short "e" items go in the net, short "i" items go in the dish, short "o" items go in the pot, and short "u" items go in the umbrella.

☆ Provide plenty of opportunities for students to change their minds and move their items if they make mistakes.

VARIATIONS

Use this activity in a learning center.

Use this activity to assess student understanding.

FOR EXAMPLE

Items to represent each vowel might include the following:

for short "a": candle, cat, mat, stamp, flag

for short "e": belt, (plastic) egg, (stuffed) pet, bell, (toy) jet

for short "i": Q-tip, stick, lid, clip

for short "o": box, sock, block, cotton, top

for short "u": gum, (toy) bus, (toy) drum, bud

GRADES: *K–2*

GROUP SIZE: *small or whole group*

WHEN TO USE: *in skills groups*

FOCUS: *short vowels*

ABCs if You Please

To your students, it seems like a treasure hunt, but this activity actually prepares children to scan information more quickly and with greater comprehension.

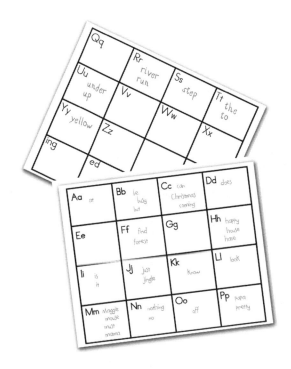

MATERIALS

Reproducible grids for recording words (see pages 60–61)

Plain white copier paper

Pencils

PREPARATION

Make one copy of each reproducible for each student.

STEP BY STEP

☆ Give each student a copy of the grids.

☆ Ask each child to look through the story for words that begin with each letter of the alphabet and to write the words he finds in the appropriate boxes. (Not every box will have a word.)

☆ Explain that students should also keep an eye out for words that end with "-ed" or "-ing" and record those in the appropriate boxes.

☆ After students complete their grids, have them discuss which words they chose, as well as which letter boxes have the fewest words and which boxes have the most.

VARIATIONS

Use this activity in a center or learning station.

Give the students a list of words to find. Have them scan the story for the words, then write inside the grid boxes each word they find and the page number on which they find it.

GRADES: *1–3*
GROUP SIZE: *individual*

WHEN TO USE: *after reading*
FOCUS: *scanning reading material*

Aa	Bb	Cc	Dd
Ee	Ff	Gg	Hh
Ii	Jj	Kk	Ll
Mm	Nn	Oo	Pp

Qq	Rr	Ss	Tt
Uu	Vv	Ww	Xx
Yy	Zz		
–ing	–ed		

Race-Car Speedway

Combine race cars with language skills for a fun way to review or to reteach skills to even the most reluctant students. Just mention the word "race" and you've got 'em!

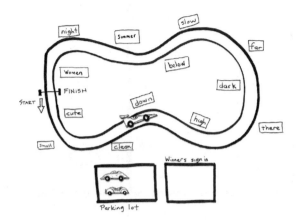

MATERIALS

Race-car reproducible (see page 63)

Plain white copier paper

Crayons

Scissors

Glue

1 magnet for each student

Magnetic chalkboard

List of 10–20 vocabulary words

PREPARATION

Make one copy of the reproducible for every three students in the class, then cut the cars apart and distribute them to students. Have each student color and cut out his race car, add his name and any designs he likes, and glue a magnet on the back. Draw a race-track on the chalkboard, and write the vocabulary words along the side of the track. At the end of the track, make a "winners' box" in which everyone can sign his name after completing the race. Next to that box, create a "parking lot" where students who have finished can park their cars. (This avoids potential distractions from students continuing to play with the cars after completing the activity.)

STEP BY STEP

☆ One at a time, have each student place his car on the starting line and then move the car around the track.

☆ Explain that each time he comes to a word, the student must stop his car and name one antonym for the word on the board before proceeding. If he's able to do that, he scores one point; if not, he moves on to the next word without gaining any points.

☆ As each student reaches the finish line, have him park his car in the "parking lot," then add his name to the "winners' box" along with the number of points he's scored.

☆ Give anyone who needs it a second chance around the track.

☆ Continue until every student has had at least one turn racing to the finish line.

VARIATIONS

Instead of focusing on antonyms, play the same game to review synonyms, abbreviations, parts of speech, contractions, or compound words.

Use chalkboard erasers for the race cars and the chalk ledge for the track. Write the words just above the chalk ledge.

For kindergarten students, replace the words with letters of the alphabet, color words, numerals, shapes, or sight words.

GRADES: *1–3*
GROUP SIZE: *4–6 students*

WHEN TO USE: *during skills groups*
FOCUS: *reviewing language skills*

Crazy Context Clues

When they come to an unknown word, young readers are apt to stop reading. Practice during skills instruction doesn't meet the needs of the hesitant reader because the bright student will almost always say the unknown word before the others have time to read on to the end of the sentence. This activity eliminates that problem by replacing the unknown word with a nonsense word. Since no one knows the meaning of the nonsense word, all students must read to the end of the sentence; the brightest student doesn't blurt out the answer and spoil things for everyone else.

Blow up the stumblelink before the party begins.

MATERIALS

5–10 sentence strips

Markers

Sticky notes

PREPARATION

Write one sentence on each strip. Leave a blank for a nonsense word in each sentence.

STEP BY STEP

☆ Ask students to make up a nonsense word like those found in a Dr. Seuss story. Let's say they come up with the nonsense word "stumblelink."

☆ Ask, "Does anyone know what a 'stumblelink' could be? Let's put it into a sentence and everyone will know what it could be."

☆ Write the word "stumblelink" on a sticky note and put the sticky note in the blank of one of your prepared sentences. For example, you might write, "Blow up the stumblelink before the party begins."

☆ Have the students read the sentence silently. Everyone will have to read to the end of the sentence to determine that a "stumblelink" is a balloon.

☆ Read the sentence aloud together.

☆ Have students discuss the strategies they used to determine the meaning of the word.

☆ Repeat the activity, inserting other nonsense words in the remaining prepared sentences.

☆ Play Crazy Context Clues several times a week. Because it's a game that can be completed very quickly, it's perfect as a meaningful activity for short blocks of time between classes or while waiting for the bus.

VARIATIONS

Use this activity in guided reading groups.

Have each student create her own nonsense words, insert each word in a sentence, and trade sentences with a partner. Have the partners attempt to determine the meaning of each other's nonsense words.

GRADES: *1–6*
GROUP SIZE: *whole group*

WHEN TO USE: *before reading*
FOCUS: *using context clues to determine meaning*

Author Map

As they read stories and books, students love learning where and when each author was born. Marking authors' birthplaces on a map teaches geography and helps students get a sense of the world beyond their community. It's a great way to get students engaged with their reading.

MATERIALS

Masking tape

1 box of sewing pins with colored balls as heads

Fine-point permanent markers

1 large world map attached to a bulletin board

List of author Web sites

PREPARATION

Fold a two-inch piece of masking tape around each sewing pin, just below the ball, to create a small flag. Keep the blank flags in a box out of student reach.

STEP BY STEP

☆ Have students use the Internet to find the birthplace and birth date of an author the class is studying. To do this, they can go to the author's Web site—or simply go to www.askjeeves.com and type in the author's name.

☆ Using a marker, write the author's name and birthday (so you can celebrate that day) on one side of a blank flag.

☆ Have the students help you find the author's birthplace on the map. Place the pin in that spot.

☆ Ask students to search the site for other information such as the author's education, size of family, etc. Discuss these discoveries with the class.

☆ Repeat the process as you study other authors. Eventually, your author map will be filled with flags marking all parts of the world.

VARIATIONS

Post a map of the United States and stick flag pins in that map as well. Students can see how many of their books are written by Americans.

Work with students to find information about each writer and post it with that person's picture next to the author map.

Make connections at the end of the year by discussing with the class what regions, countries, or continents most of our authors come from.

FOR EXAMPLE

Many contemporary authors have their own Web sites. Here are a few examples to get you started.

Author	Web site
Avi	www.avi-writer.com
Judy Blume	www.judyblume.com
Jan Brett	www.janbrett.com
Eric Carle	www.eric-carle.com
Robert Munsch	www.robertmunsch.com
Patricia Polacco	www.patriciapolacco.com
Many authors	www.childrenslit.com

GRADES: *2–6*
GROUP SIZE: *whole group*

WHEN TO USE: *before, during & after reading*
FOCUS: *making a connection between author & story*

Extra! Extra! Read All About It!

This activity develops the skill of synthesizing—using existing information to create something new. In this case, students use a newspaper format to visually demonstrate their comprehension of nonfiction material. It's a terrific assessment tool.

MATERIALS

1 ruler for each student

1 sheet of white drawing paper (12" X 18") for each student

Pencils and crayons

STEP BY STEP

☆ Have each student use her ruler to draw a frame inside the edges of her paper.

☆ Ask the student to position her paper with the short side at the top. Direct her to draw a straight line across the top of the paper, placing the line a ruler's width below the frame. This allows space for a topic headline.

☆ Have the student use the ruler to divide the remainder of the paper inside the frame into four or six (depending on grade level) boxes, all the same size. The format should resemble the front page of a newspaper.

☆ Instruct the student to use information she's learned from her reading to make a report in each square. Each report could be in the form of a graph, a list, a map, a diagram, or all of these.

☆ Explain that each section should include a headline and written information. There should be at least one illustration.

☆ Use the completed project to assess the student's comprehension of the material.

VARIATIONS

Use this same newspaper format for content-area information.

Use this same format with math topics. You might ask a student to demonstrate his knowledge of fractions, geometry, or measurement in the newspaper grid.

Use this format as an alternative to a traditional book report.

GRADES: *2–6*
GROUP SIZE: *individual*

WHEN TO USE: *after reading*
FOCUS: *synthesizing nonfiction information*

The Powerful Apostrophe

A simple drawing activity makes the use of the apostrophe easy to understand.

MATERIALS

Dog reproducible (see page 68)

Basket-of-cats reproducible (see page 69)

Plain white copier paper

Markers

Pencils

PREPARATION

Make one copy of each of the two reproducibles for each student, plus one enlarged copy of each.

STEP BY STEP

☆ Model for students with the large copy of the dog reproducible while students follow your example on their copies. Point out that this is one dog but that he is the owner of several things.

☆ Elicit suggestions from the students as to what things might belong to the dog. This could be part of the dog's body (his tail or his ear) or something else that belongs to him (a bone or a bowl).

☆ If necessary, add to the drawing anything the students suggest that's not already included. For each thing the students name, add a label with the word "dog's" and then draw an arrow from the label to the item mentioned. For example, if students suggested including the tail, you'd write "dog's tail" and then draw an arrow pointing to the tail. If someone suggested the bowl, you'd draw that into the picture as students did the same on their copies. Then you'd write "dog's bowl," with an arrow pointing to it.

☆ Continue until you've included and labeled ten things belonging to the dog. The class might suggest collar, leg, nose, ball, food, doghouse, ear, bone, paw, and tail.

☆ Emphasize the use of the apostrophe and "s" to show possession with a singular noun.

☆ Collect papers so you can use them for a comparison lesson later.

☆ Continue the lesson on another day. Follow the same procedure as above, but start with the reproducible of the basket of cats. Point out that there are several cats and that they share many things.

☆ Elicit suggestions as to what they might share. Students might suggest food, for example, or a basket.

☆ If students suggest items that aren't already in the drawing, add those things to the drawing. Label each one, using the apostrophe appropriately, then draw an arrow from the label to the item mentioned. For example, you and the students might draw a picture of "cats' food" with an arrow pointing from the label to the food.

☆ Continue until you have labeled ten things the cats share.

☆ Emphasize the use of the "s" and apostrophe to show possession with a plural noun.

☆ Compare the drawings from the two lessons and discuss strategies for using the apostrophe to show possession with singular and plural nouns.

GRADES: *K–3*

GROUP SIZE: *whole group*

WHEN TO USE: *during skills groups*

FOCUS: *using apostrophes with possessive nouns*

Presentation Helpers

Take the anxiety out of oral presentations with these simple presentation helpers.

MATERIALS

1 inflatable microphone (available through online novelty stores) or an inexpensive real microphone

1 music stand

1 sugarless lollipop for each student (optional)

STEP BY STEP

☆ When a student presents a report or story he's written, give him a microphone to hold. This puts the focus on the individual student, promoting self-esteem, and seems to relax nervous students.

☆ In addition, allow students to place their work on an inexpensive music stand as they give their presentations. The music stand is too light for students to lean on but gives them space for papers and presentation aids.

☆ When students are presenting their own written work in round-robin form as part of a presentation circle, another option is to give each student a sugarless lollipop. Explain that when the student reads his piece, he can use the lollipop as a microphone. Meanwhile, the other students may quietly suck on their lollipops to minimize talking.

TEACHER TIP

If you have a hard time locating an inexpensive music stand, ask your music teacher to lend you one.

GRADES: *2–6*
GROUP SIZE: *small group or whole group*

WHEN TO USE: *during student presentations*
FOCUS: *language development through oral presentation*

_____
title

_____ _____
Name two characters and circle one.

_____ _____ _____
Write three words to describe the character you circled.

_____ _____ _____ _____
Name four settings from the book and circle one.

_____ _____ _____
Write three words to describe the setting you circled.

_____ _____
Name the type of story or book this is.

_____
Write one word that tells how you felt at the end.

Goal Bracelet

Making a goal bracelet and wearing it every day helps a student learn to set goals and keeps him focused on achieving those goals.

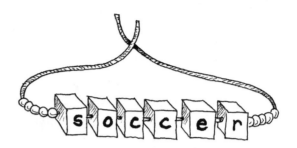

MATERIALS

Construction paper in dark colors

Tape

1-foot section of stretch plastic bracelet string per child

Plain paper

Pencils

Large bags of plain plastic colored beads, and beads with imprinted letters

PREPARATION

First you need to make the clear plastic bracelet string stand out so children can see it. To do this, tape construction paper to each child's desk; then tape one end of the bracelet string to the construction paper.

STEP BY STEP

☆ Talk with students about setting goals. Explain the meaning of the word "goal" and discuss with students the steps one can take to achieve a goal. Be sure to explain that it's important to revisit a goal often to determine if one is making progress toward achieving it. Also explain the meanings of long-term and short-term goals.

☆ Encourage each student to choose a long-term goal for the year and to determine one or two words that will remind him of that goal. If a child determines that he wants to become a better soccer player, he might choose the word "soccer."

☆ Assist the students in writing down the steps they'll need to take to achieve their goals.

FOR EXAMPLE

A student who decides she wants to improve her reading skills might choose the words "better reader." Before making a goal bracelet using those words, she might write on her paper something like this:

<u>Steps to Becoming a Better Reader</u>

Read more often.

Read lots of books that I enjoy.

Have my mom or dad read aloud to me.

Read out loud to my mom or dad.

Set aside a time each day to read.

GRADES: *2–6*
GROUP SIZE: *small group, large group, or individual*

WHEN TO USE: *at the beginning of the school year*
FOCUS: *goal setting*

☆ Have the students choose the letter beads they need for the word(s) that describe their goals, then begin making their goal bracelets.

☆ To start a bracelet, have each student place five to seven plain beads on the string, followed by the letter beads that make up the goal word(s). He can then add five to seven more plain beads to complete the bracelet.

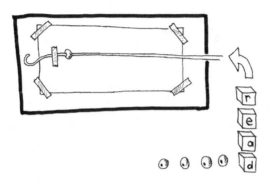

☆ Ask each student to carefully detach the string from the construction paper and tie the ends together with a knot. Check to be sure each bracelet fits its owner's wrist snugly; the stretchy string makes it easy to remove. (Some students may need to remove any plain beads that make their bracelets too large.)

☆ Encourage students to wear their bracelets often to remind them of their goals and the steps they must take to achieve those goals.

☆ Conduct a weekly goal discussion in which students tell how they worked toward achieving their goals that week.

TEACHER TIP

Beads and bracelet string can be purchased at craft stores and through online novelty companies.

VARIATIONS

Use plain beads in place of the letter beads, and have each student write letters on the beads with a fine-point permanent marker.

Have students use regular string to make goal necklaces.

Make the goals specific to one area of students' lives. For example, you may want the students to identify school-related goals or family-related goals.

What's in a Name?

Students develop research skills as well as an appreciation of their names with this fun beginning-of-the-year activity. It also helps you learn about your students and their interests.

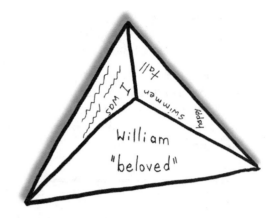

MATERIALS

1 copy of the book *Chrysanthemum*, by Kevin Henkes

1 sheet of 8 ½" X 8 ½" paper for each student

Scissors

Pencils

Glue sticks

Several books with origins of names

STEP BY STEP

☆ On the first day of school, read *Chrysanthemum* to the students.

☆ Discuss names and how every person's name is part of what makes him unique.

☆ Explain that each student's assignment is to ask his parents how he got his first name.

☆ The next day, hand out the paper, scissors, pencils, and glue sticks.

☆ Model for students how to make a triarama (see directions on page 77).

☆ Ask each student to create a triarama to display information about himself.

☆ After they've cut and folded their sheets of paper, instruct students to unfold their papers and lay them flat so they can write easily on the triangles.

☆ On the first triangle, instruct each student to write his first name. Then he should find the meaning of his name in one of the name books and write the meaning below his name. A child named William might write "beloved," a boy named Craig might write "cave dweller," etc.

☆ Explain that on the second triangle, the student should write how he got his name. For example, someone might write, "I was named Jonathan because that is my grandfather's name."

☆ On the third triangle, ask each student to write a list of words that describe him. He might write "short," "bike rider," "wears glasses," etc.

☆ Have each child assemble his triarama, glue it together, and place it on his desk.

VARIATIONS

Collect and stack the completed triaramas so substitutes can use them to learn student names.

Older students can research their last names and record genealogical information on the triaramas.

Have students make acronym-style poems based on their names and write the poems on their triaramas in lieu of the descriptions. For example, Sam might write, S – silly, A – always late, M – magnificent!

GRADES: *2–6*
GROUP SIZE: *whole group followed by students working individually*

WHEN TO USE: *after reading*
FOCUS: *working with words*

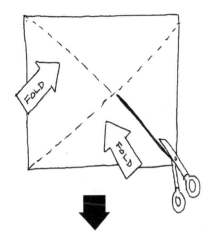

How to Make a Triarama

1. Take a square sheet of paper and fold it in half diagonally. Then fold it diagonally again, creating four triangles. Open the sheet of paper and cut along one of the fold lines, cutting from the corner just to the center.

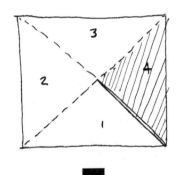

2. Write on three of the triangles, but leave the fourth one (the one to the right of the cut) blank.

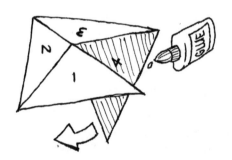

3. Assemble the triarama by gluing the first triangle on top of the fourth one, creating a miniature pyramid shape.

Fun Fan

The Fun Fan offers a simple, organized way to manipulate spelling words. And the sticks can be used over and over again to manipulate other sets of words in other ways.

MATERIALS

20 large craft sticks for each student

Drill

1 small, clear, plastic freezer bag for each student

Permanent marker

1 wing nut for each student

1 bolt (1 ½"–2") for each student

1 wooden (not mechanical) pencil for each student

One 1" square gum eraser for each student

List of 20 spelling words

PREPARATION

In the end of each craft stick, drill a hole the same diameter as the bolt. Write the name of a student in permanent marker on the outside of the freezer bag and place twenty craft sticks inside the bag, along with a wing nut, bolt, pencil, and eraser. Repeat this procedure for each student in the class.

STEP BY STEP

☆ Write the spelling words on the chalkboard.

☆ Give each student one of the plastic bags.

☆ Ask each student to use the pencil to write one spelling word on each of his sticks.

☆ Explain that each child is to place his word sticks in alphabetical order, then put the sticks on the bolt and hold them together with the wing nut.

☆ Ask students to fan out the individual sticks so you can assess alphabetization skills at a glance.

☆ When you're ready for students to work with other words, have them erase this set and start over with the new words.

VARIATIONS

Instead of (or after) placing the words in alphabetical order, have each student rearrange them, dividing the words into groups according to the number of syllables they contain.

Substitute vocabulary words for spelling words, completing the activity in the same way.

Write math problems on the board or a sheet of paper, then have students solve the problems and write their answers on the sticks. Have them assemble the sticks into the Fun Fan, retaining the order in which the questions were asked. It's easy to check the answers by fanning out the sticks.

Have students write a part of a story on each stick, then assign other students to sequence the sticks to match the order of events in the story.

GRADES: *2–6*
GROUP SIZE: *individual*

WHEN TO USE: *during spelling or vocabulary lesson*
FOCUS: *alphabetical order*

Word-Nas-Tics

When they physically demonstrate how letters work together to form specific words, students build understanding and move spellings into long-term memory.

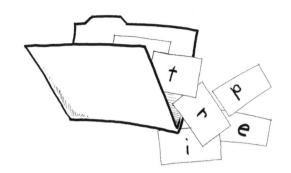

MATERIALS

Short list of vocabulary words

Paper

Marker

1 manila folder per group

PREPARATION

Choose words that match the unit of study. You might use words that include consonant blends, short and long vowels, contractions, etc. Write the individual letters for each word on separate sheets of paper and place the lettered sheets inside a manila folder. Use one letter per sheet and one folder per word. (The total number of letters needs to equal the number of students who are participating. So if you have twenty-one students in the class, you might have three five-letter words and one six-letter word.)

STEP BY STEP

☆ Divide the students into groups so that the number of students in each group matches the number of letters in the word you're about to give them.

☆ Give each group its folder.

☆ Have each student in the group take one letter from the folder.

☆ Ask students to group themselves together to spell the word correctly, and to show how the letters work together in that particular word.

> ### FOR EXAMPLE
>
> *For the word "stripe," the first three students might put their arms around each other's shoulders, indicating that the first three letters combine for the initial blend "str." The next student might stand on his toes to indicate the long vowel "i." The next child might form the letter "p" with his hand on his hip. And the last student might hold his hand over his mouth to indicate a silent "e."*

☆ Give each group praise and applause.

☆ Follow up with a class discussion about each group's strategies.

VARIATIONS

Have the group make a drawing together rather than using their bodies to demonstrate the sounds in the word.

Share your Word-Nas-Tics with other classes and challenge them to figure out which strategies the students used.

GRADES: *1–6*
GROUP SIZE: *small groups, followed by whole group*

WHEN TO USE: *during skills groups*
FOCUS: *phonics*

Show Me

Meet the needs of all students, especially the tactile/kinesthetic learners, with this interactive, individualized tool. This activity also gives you a way to assess each student's understanding of vocabulary words.

MATERIALS

Glue

1 strip (1 ½" X 9 ½") colored tagboard for each student

1 report-card envelope (6 ½" X 9 ½") for each student

List of 8–12 vocabulary words

8–12 small pieces of colored tagboard (roughly 3" X 5" or smaller) for each child

Pencils

TEACHER TIP

We've found it helpful to use four different colors of tagboard for this activity, and to make sure that the color of each student's tagboard strip matches the color of her vocabulary cards. This saves lots of confusion when those cards fall on the floor!

STEP BY STEP

☆ Preparing the envelope is in itself a great lesson in listening and following directions. Explain to the class that each student is to glue her tagboard strip to the bottom edge of the front of the envelope. Add that she should glue only the bottom and the two ends to the envelope; she's to leave the top part open, forming a pocket. She should not seal the flap of the envelope.

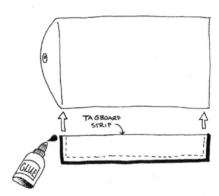

☆ Write the vocabulary words on the chalkboard, and have each student copy one vocabulary word onto each of her tagboard cards, leaving some blank space at the bottom of the card. (If you prefer, you can do this yourself ahead of time.) All students should have the same words on their sets of cards.

GRADES: *K–3*
GROUP SIZE: *whole group*

WHEN TO USE: *before & after reading*
FOCUS: *vocabulary recognition & association*

☆ At this point, you may want to collect the folders and laminate them for increased durability. If you do this, you'll need to then cut two slits in the lamination. Cut one slit to re-create the opening for the tagboard pocket; then flip the envelope over and cut another slit in the lamination to allow access to the inside of the envelope. Return the folders to their owners.

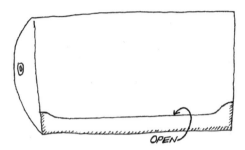

OPEN

☆ Have students spread their word cards out in front of them.

☆ Explain that when you call out one of the words, each student is to pick up that word and place it in the pocket she made on the front of her envelope. She should then hold the pocket under her chin, with the word facing her so no one can see it.

☆ Wait until all envelopes are under the students' chins. Then say, "Show me."

☆ Explain that when you give that command, the students are to turn their envelopes around, each child showing her word but still keeping the envelope under her chin. Having students hold the cards this way helps you to see when all students are ready (when they have the words under their chins but facing them) and make observations for quick assessment (after they turn the cards around). It also keeps word cards from flying out of the pockets and getting mixed with other students' words.

☆ Allow the students to take turns being the teacher and calling out the words.

☆ Have each student store his word cards for the week inside his envelope.

VARIATIONS

This is a good homework tool to share with parents. Have each student make two Show Me envelopes, one for school and one to take home. Be sure to send home directions for parents, along with a list of words for the week.

To use the same activity for content areas, have students write names, dates, or content vocabulary words on the cards.

Have each student make two sets of ten numerals (0 through 9) each. Use these for practice in building three- and four-place numerals; reviewing addition, subtraction, and multiplication facts; building fact families; and showing answers to word problems.

Have students write spelling words on cards, then cut the cards apart and rebuild the words in the Show Me pocket.

Give each student the letters for one large word and ask her to use those letters to build smaller words in the Show Me pocket.

Play matching games with the Show Me envelope. Prepare pairs of pictures and words, synonyms, antonyms, rhyming words, contractions, numerals and sets, or words and definitions. Have students put the pairs in the Show Me pockets.

Towels for Vowels

Hand towels and paper towels become classroom tools—and add a bit of extra interest—as students switch vowels to create new words.

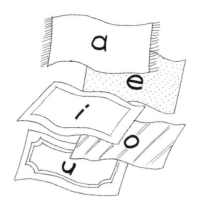

MATERIALS

Fabric paint

5 hand towels

1 paper towel for each student

1 blank overhead transparency

1 overhead projector

Dry-erase markers

Crayons or permanent markers

PREPARATION

Use fabric paint to write one vowel on each of the five hand towels.

STEP BY STEP

☆ Divide the class into two teams.

☆ Give each student an unfolded paper towel.

☆ Place the hand towels on a table in the front of the class, vowel-side up.

☆ Begin the game by writing a word on the overhead transparency and the same word on the chalkboard.

☆ Challenge a student from Team A to create a new word by changing or adding one or more vowels to the word written on the overhead. So if the original word was "bat," she might change it to "but" or "bait."

☆ Explain that the student must take to the overhead the hand towel(s) with the new vowel(s).

She should either replace the previous vowel, add another one, or do both to make a new word. (She can use a wet paper towel to erase any letters she's replacing.) Then she should add her new word to the list on the chalkboard and return her hand towel(s) to the table. For example, if the original word was "star," the student might pick up the "e" towel and then create the word "stare," or she might take the "i" towel and then change "star" to "stir."

☆ Give Team A one point if the student successfully creates a new word by changing or adding one or more vowels.

☆ Explain that all students, including the one who created the new word, should use crayons or markers to record the new word on their paper towels.

☆ Ask the first member of Team B to repeat the process, starting from the word on the transparency.

☆ Continue the game with the teams taking turns creating new words.

☆ When students have exhausted all possibilities for new words, write a new starting word on the transparency and chalkboard. Continue the process until every student has had a turn.

VARIATION

To offer practice in counting money, attach monetary values to the vowels and have students track the total. For example, an "a" might be worth a nickel, an "e" two pennies, an "i" a dime, etc. Use real coins.

GRADES: *1–3*
GROUP SIZE: *whole group*
WHEN TO USE: *during skills groups*
FOCUS: *distinguishing vowel sounds*

82   **TEACH THE WAY THEY LEARN**

Beanie Boosters

A few beans can help a student master and identify words that are often confused. The visual and physical nature of this activity makes it a favorite strategy for students—and an effective one, too.

MATERIALS

1 sheet of 9" X 12" tagboard for each student

Marker

1 paper cup for each student

Packages of dried navy, kidney, black, pinto, and great northern beans (available at large grocery stores)

White glue

PREPARATION

On each sheet of tagboard, write two to six similar words (e.g., "to," "too," and "two") that you want the class to study. Pour several different types of beans into each paper cup.

FOR EXAMPLE

Words you might want to consider for this activity include:

to, too, two

where, what, when, why

there, their, them, that

though, through, thought

our, hour, your

was, saw

STEP BY STEP

☆ Distribute the tagboard and the cups of beans to the students.

☆ Have students read the words on the tagboard aloud together.

☆ Ask each student to outline the letters of each word with glue and then put the beans on the glue. Explain that students are to use a different kind of bean for each word.

VARIATIONS

Use this activity in a center or work station.

This can be a good differentiated activity, giving each student a chance to practice words that are difficult for him. Students who consistently write a letter or word backwards, for example, can benefit from this practice.

GRADES: *K–3*
GROUP SIZE: *individual*

WHEN TO USE: *during skills groups*
FOCUS: *word identification & spelling*

Flip a Word

Identifying several different relationships for a word helps students to master both meaning and spelling.

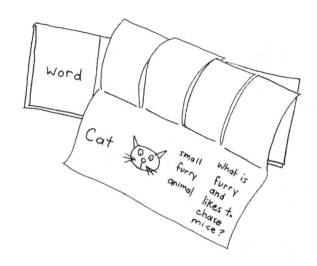

MATERIALS

1 sheet of 8 ½" X 11" paper per student per word

Scissors

Colored markers or pencils

List of vocabulary or spelling words

1 dictionary for each student

1 zippered plastic sandwich bag for each student

STEP BY STEP

☆ Give each student one sheet of paper per vocabulary or spelling word.

☆ Have the child make a flip book by folding the paper in half vertically, then making three evenly spaced cuts (creating four flaps) from the long edge of the paper just to the fold.

☆ Instruct the student to write "word" on the first of the flaps, "picture" on the second, "definition" on the third, and "clue question" on the fourth.

☆ Give students a word from your list. Explain that under the "word" flap, the student is to use colored markers or pencils to write the word.

☆ Under the "picture" flap, she should draw a picture that makes a connection for her. For example, for the word "cat" she might draw whiskers or a ball of yarn.

☆ "Definition" is next. Ask the student to look up the definition in the dictionary and then write it in her own words under this flap.

☆ Under the "clue" flap, the student is to write a question for which the answer is the word she's studying. For example, for the word "cat," a student might write, "What is furry and likes to chase mice?"

☆ Have students repeat the process for each of their other words until every child has made a Flip-a-Word booklet for each word.

☆ Have students share their booklets with other students.

☆ Ask students to fold their Flip-a-Word sets and store them in zippered plastic sandwich bags.

☆ Encourage students to use the Flip-a-Word booklets during SSR or quiet reading time to help them retain both the spelling and the meaning of their words.

VARIATIONS

Assign students to four groups and ask each group to complete five booklets. If you like, duplicate each booklet on a copy machine so each student can have a copy.

Use this same strategy to reinforce content vocabulary.

GRADES: *2–6*
GROUP SIZE: *individual*

WHEN TO USE: *during skills groups*
FOCUS: *spelling & determining meaning*

Step on It!

Brain-based learning research suggests that incorporating movement with learning leads to maximum retention. Students practice thinking on their feet in this fast-paced working-with-words activity.

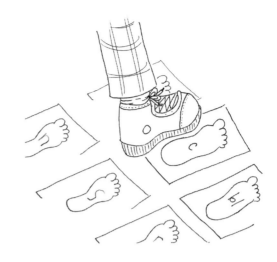

MATERIALS

Footprint reproducible (see page 86)

3 sheets of 9" X 12" tagboard per student

Markers

List of 12 letters, sounds, or words

PREPARATION

Cut each sheet of tagboard in half so that you have two sheets, each measuring 9" X 6". For each student, you'll need six of these half-sheets with a footprint on each side of each sheet. You can create these by making double-sided copies of the reproducible, drawing a footprint on each half-sheet, or having the students draw or trace their own feet. On each footprint, write one letter, sound, or word to be practiced. Use both the fronts and the backs so you can include twelve different letters or words in each set. Give each student a set of the same letters or words.

STEP BY STEP

☆ Have each student stand and place the six footprints on the floor in front of her, arranged in two rows of three footprints each. Be sure to tell students which letters, etc. they should have facing up at the beginning of the game, so everyone's working with the same choices.

☆ Call out a letter, sound, or word from your list, and ask students to step on it simultaneously in response. Explain that as they step on the footprints, they should repeat: "Step on it. Step on it. Ready, set, go. Step on the 'c.' It's a letter we know." Or "Step on 'bl.' It's a blend we know." Or "Step on 'where.' It's a word we know."

☆ After you've been through all the letters, sounds, or words on one side of the footprints, have students turn them over and repeat the game.

VARIATIONS

Write numbers on the cards, then call out word problems. Have students mentally work the problem and then step on the answer.

Write contractions, suffixes, prefixes, or parts of speech on the cards. Call out examples. Ask students to respond by stepping on the appropriate cards.

GRADES: *K–3*
GROUP SIZE: *6–12 students*

WHEN TO USE: *during skills groups*
FOCUS: *letter, sound & word recognition*

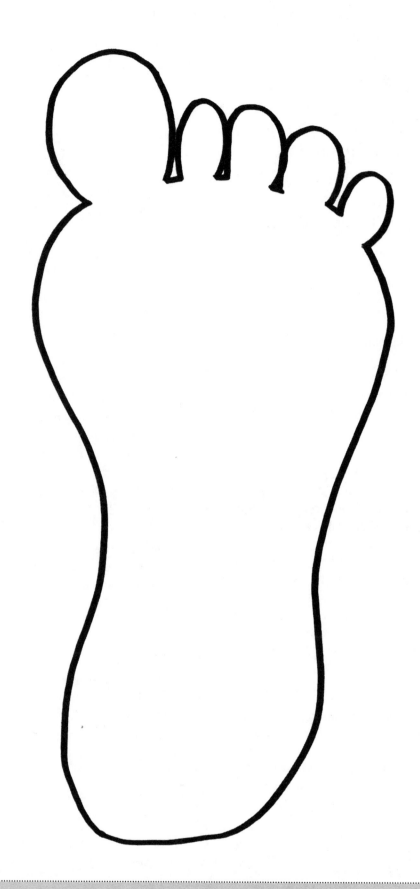

We See Spots

See a spot and make a match! This quick eye-hand-coordination game offers an engaging, effective way to teach letter and sound recognition.

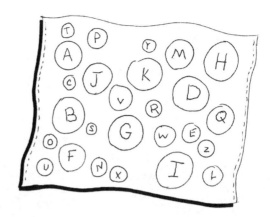

MATERIALS

Plain tablecloth, plastic or vinyl, in any color (available inexpensively at discount department stores)

Circle patterns in 2 sizes

1 black permanent marker

Reproducibles for alphabet letters (see pages 88–91)

Plain white copier paper

PREPARATION

Cut the tablecloth in half. Trace the circle patterns on the tablecloth with the permanent marker, making sure you have twenty-six circles on each half tablecloth. In random order, write one uppercase alphabet letter in each circle. Make two copies of each reproducible. Cut the copies apart, so you have a total of fifty-two pieces (two copies of each letter).

STEP BY STEP

☆ Spread one set of letters around the edge of each tablecloth.

☆ Divide students into two groups of two to eight students each. Seat students on the floor with one group around each half tablecloth.

☆ Call out a letter, then ask, "Who will spot it?"

☆ One of the students finds that letter and places it on the matching letter on the tablecloth.

VARIATIONS

Call out a word. The student who has the beginning letter or ending letter of that word should "spot it," matching his letter to the appropriate one on the tablecloth.

Write numbers on the circles. Create student cards with problems, coins, or sets on them, and play the game as described above.

Write abbreviations on the circles. Give students cards with the matching words.

> ## TEACHER TIP
>
> *Plates and saucers make good templates for drawing the circles on the tablecloth halves. If you use some with a five-inch diameter and some with a three-inch diameter, you'll have enough variety to make this look more like a game. Including the three-inch circles will also let you fit all twenty-six letters on each half tablecloth.*

GRADES: *K–2*
GROUP SIZE: *2–8 students in each of 2 groups*

WHEN TO USE: *during skills groups*
FOCUS: *letter & sound recognition*

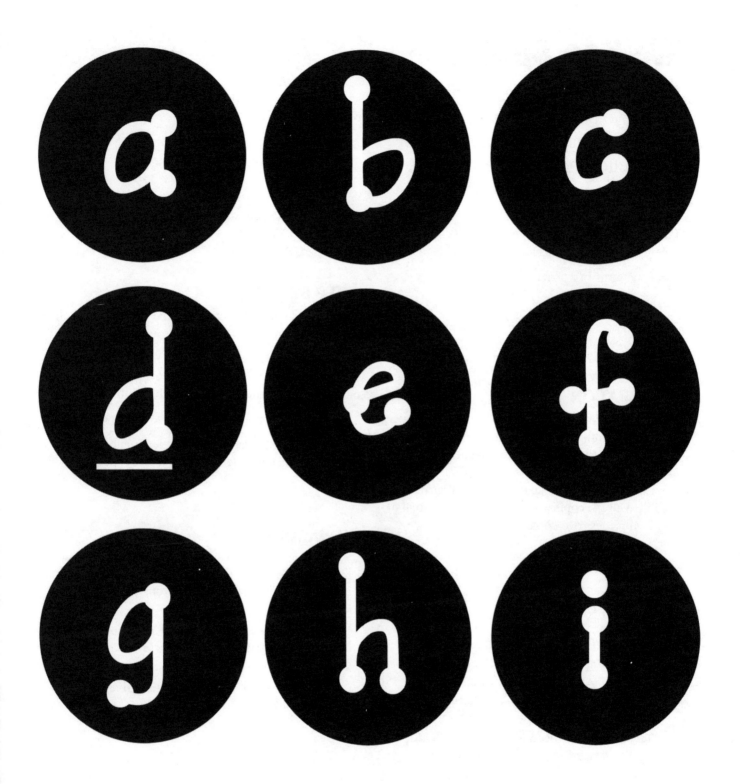

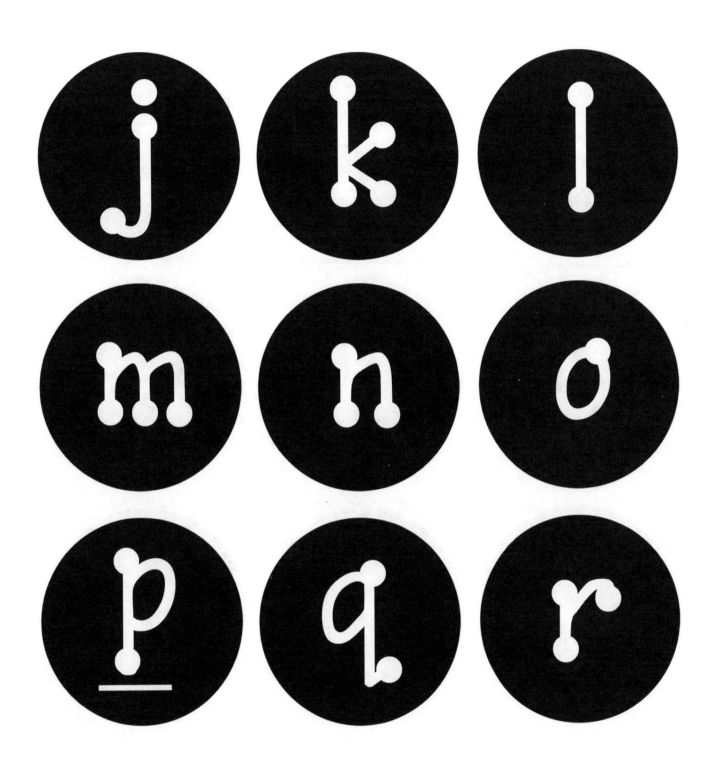

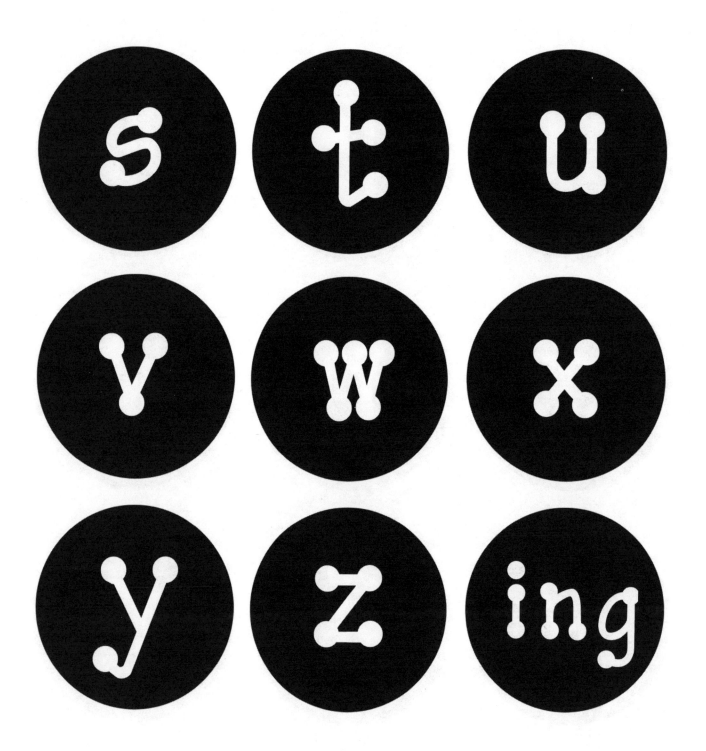

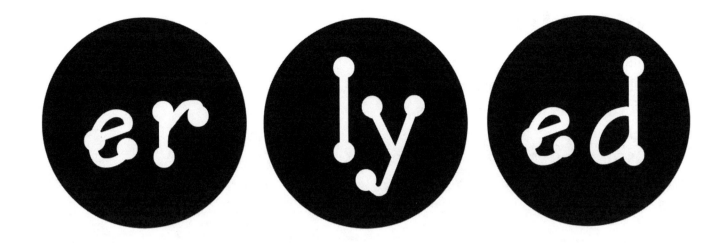

Quizboard

In this activity, colors help students maintain their places; they also establish focal points for you. Students like the Quizboard because it eliminates stress for them; you'll like it because it's such an easy and effective assessment tool.

MATERIALS

1 sheet of poster board

Markers in several colors

List of words to be reviewed

PREPARATION

Create a chart on the poster board by writing five words in each of several rows, using a different color for every row. These can be vocabulary words, sight words, or words in phonetic groups.

STEP BY STEP

☆ Have students seated on the floor.

☆ As you hold the chart in front of them, ask students to focus on a certain line (e.g., the line written in blue). Ask students to find a particular word in that line, and to indicate their responses by holding their fingers under their chins. For instance, if the word you called was the second word on the line, each student would respond by holding two fingers under his chin. If the word called was the fourth word on the line, each student should respond by holding four fingers under his chin.

☆ Next, extend the assessment to include association. Ask students to find the word that begins like "frog" or ends like "slowly." Or give a meaning, antonym, or synonym for each of the words on the chart. Each time the students respond with fingers only.

☆ As you observe the responses, you'll see who's mastered the words as well as who needs more practice.

VARIATIONS

For math assessment, write numbers on the chart and call out problems.

For social-studies assessment, write names and call out dates, or vice versa.

Shh! It's a Secret

It's easy for students to remember difficult words or facts if you turn the information into an interactive game and call it a secret!

MATERIALS

1 sticky note for each student

Plain white paper

Pencils

STEP BY STEP

☆ Provide each student with one sticky note.

☆ Ask each child to write "secret" across his sticky note and attach the note to a piece of paper.

☆ Have the student lift the edge of the sticky note and write on the paper, under the note, a word or group of words you provide. This "secret" should be something that causes confusion and difficulty in your classroom. For example, you might ask students to write the word "through"; the homonyms "too," "two," and "to"; the letters "b" and "d"; or the words "was" and "saw."

☆ Tell your students that the word(s) under the note will be the class secret for the week and that by the end of the week, the secret won't be a problem for anyone in the class.

☆ Every day, all week long, stop periodically and refer to the secret.

☆ On one day, ask students to write the secret in the air.

☆ The next day, ask them to turn their papers upside down and write the secret in the smallest handwriting possible.

☆ Later, have each child write the secret on her neighbor's back with one finger.

☆ Another time, tell students to close their eyes and spell the secret softly.

☆ Later, ask each child to whisper the secret to the person in front of her in line.

☆ Finally, ask a student to write the secret with purple chalk in the highest place she can reach on the chalkboard.

☆ All of this attention to one problem causes familiarity, which leads to mastery—not to mention fun—for everyone. By the end of the week, everyone knows the "secret."

VARIATIONS

Make the secret a hard-to-remember math fact, such as $6 + 8 = 14$.

Choose a difficult date (e.g., 1776) or vocabulary word (e.g., "photosynthesis") from a content area and make it the secret.

GRADES: *4–6*
GROUP SIZE: *whole group*

WHEN TO USE: *in skills groups*
FOCUS: *mastering difficult words & facts*

Five Fabulous Phonics Minutes

In five short minutes every morning, students practice and learn some of the key elements of phonetic skills. You can also use this for a quick assessment.

MATERIALS

List of 1–3 phonics skills for the day

STEP BY STEP

☆ Start a lively rally of verbal prompts with a question that requires one of the skills you've selected. If you're focusing on rhyming, you might say, "Which word doesn't rhyme with the other two? 'Big,' 'fig,' or 'tug'?" (Using verbal prompts rather than written ones helps students discriminate among the sounds.)

☆ Encourage students to respond quickly, calling out the answers (in this case "tug") together. Or call on an individual student to respond to each prompt.

VARIATIONS

Rather than having them respond orally, have students write their answers.

Write the prompts on the board so students can practice visual discrimination.

FOR EXAMPLE

Vowel Sounds

Which of these words have the same vowel sound? <u>CAT</u>, THINK, <u>BAD</u>

Which vowel sound does each of these words have? LIGHT, ICE, SKYLIGHT (long "i")

Prefixes

Of these words, which two have prefixes? CHAIR, <u>UNFRIENDLY</u>, <u>DISAGREE</u>

Suffixes

Which of these words does not have a suffix? PLAYED, CRYING, <u>MANY</u>

Consonant Sounds

Which of these words have the same consonant blend sounds? <u>CHURCH</u>, SHELF, <u>CHILD</u>

Which word does not belong? SKIP, <u>STEP</u>, SKETCH

GRADES: *K–6*   **WHEN TO USE:** *before reading & during skills groups*
GROUP SIZE: *whole group*   **FOCUS:** *working with words*

94   TEACH THE WAY THEY LEARN

Spelling Bingo

With this new twist on an old game, students don't just practice their spelling words; they truly learn them.

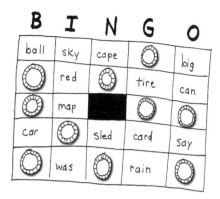

MATERIALS

Bingo-card reproducible (see page 96)

Card stock

Clipboard

Plain white paper

Pencil

List of up to 24 spelling words

24 beans, pennies, or bingo chips for each student

PREPARATION

Using the card stock, make one copy of the reproducible for each student. Set up a clipboard with the list of spelling words, so that you can check them off as you go.

STEP BY STEP

☆ Have each student write the spelling words on her bingo card in random order. (The card has twenty-four spaces for words, so if the word list has fewer than twenty-four words, students may need to repeat some of the words.)

☆ Hand out whatever you're using for markers.

☆ Call out the words as you would call out numbers in a traditional bingo game. As you call out each word, check it off on your clipboard list.

☆ Explain that each student is to cover the words on his card as you call them.

☆ Continue the game until a student has a marker on every box in one column. At that point the student calls out "Bingo!"

FOR EXAMPLE

Try giving word clues based on any of the following (or based on any combination of the following):

- spelling backward
- number of syllables
- definitions
- prefixes or suffixes
- vowel sounds
- consonant sounds
- how the words begin and end
- spelling (You spell the word and the students find it on their cards.)

☆ Ask the student with the winning card to read back the list of words, confirming that he's correct.

☆ Play again, but this time add new twists. Rather than calling out the words themselves, give clues. For example, for the word "bicycle," you might say, "This word has a prefix. It has three syllables and begins with the second letter of the alphabet."

VARIATION

Substitute numbers for words on the bingo cards, then read math problems or equations. Have students mark the numbers that answer the problems.

GRADES: *2–6*
GROUP SIZE: *whole group*

WHEN TO USE: *in spelling groups*
FOCUS: *spelling*

B I N G O

		■		

Royal Spellers

This royal twist on an old-fashioned spelling bee is perfect for reviewing large lists of spelling words.

MATERIALS

2 paper crowns

List of 30–50 spelling words (e.g., a unit or quarterly review list)

PREPARATION

Set up two thrones (chairs) at the front of the classroom, facing the class.

STEP BY STEP

☆ Divide the class into two or three teams. Let's say you have Team A and Team B.

☆ Ask each team to choose a person to be their king or queen for the first round. Give each ruler a crown to wear.

☆ Have the crowned rulers take their royal places on thrones.

☆ Give the king of Team A one word to spell, and explain that he may choose to write it on the chalkboard or spell it orally. If he spells it correctly, he gains a point for his team.

☆ Repeat the process, giving the queen of Team B a different word to spell.

☆ Continue, giving each ruler one word at a time, until one of the rulers fails to spell his word correctly.

☆ When someone misspells a word, his team does not get a point. The king steps down and chooses another member of his team to be king for the team's next turn.

☆ Continue the game until all words have been used or until time runs out.

VARIATIONS

Review math facts with this strategy, substituting problems for the words.

To give students practice with tallying, have them use tally marks to keep track of the score.

GRADES: *K–3*
GROUP SIZE: *whole group*

WHEN TO USE: *during spelling*
FOCUS: *spelling review*

Riddle Sticks

Students show and reinforce their understanding of phonetic relationships as they write, trade, and solve riddles for spelling words.

MATERIALS

40–50 spelling words

1 small index card for each group

Marker

Tagboard (approximately one 9" X 12" sheet per group)

Scissors

1 tall potato-chip can for each group

1 sheet of notebook paper for each student

Pencils

PREPARATION

Decide how many groups will be participating. Create a different list of spelling review words for each group, with each list consisting of ten words. Write one of the lists on each index card. Cut ten strips of tagboard per list, each approximately 1" X 9". If you like, decorate the outside of each can. Place one of the lists of spelling words in each can, along with ten of the blank strips of tagboard. These strips will become the Riddle Sticks.

STEP BY STEP

☆ Divide students into four to five groups. Give each group one of the cans you've prepared.

☆ Ask each group to take one of the "sticks" and to choose one word from their list. Explain that their assignment is to write the number of the word (from the index card) on the stick and then to work together to figure out three clues for that word. They should then write their clues on the stick.

☆ Have the groups continue choosing words and writing clues for each word on their lists.

☆ When they've finished giving clues for all the words on their list, ask each group to place their index card and the sticks with the clues inside the can.

☆ Ask the groups to trade cans and solve the riddles. Hand out one sheet of notebook paper to each student. Explain that each member of the group should number his paper from one to ten and record his answers on that paper.

☆ When they finish writing their responses, encourage students in each group to check their answers against the list of words on the index card inside the can.

> ## FOR EXAMPLE
>
> *For the word "blue," students might write clues something like these:*
>
> *1. I am a color.*
>
> *2. I rhyme with "glue."*
>
> *3. I begin with the sound "bl."*

Circle Spelling

Strengthen spelling, sequencing, and listening skills while giving students a chance to be up and moving with a purpose.

MATERIALS

List of spelling words for review

STEP BY STEP

☆ Ask students to stand in a circle.

☆ Designate a student to be the starter.

☆ Call out one spelling word.

☆ Ask the starter to give the first letter of that word orally.

☆ Have the student to the starter's left give the next letter of the word.

☆ Continue the process, with one student giving each letter, until all the letters of the word have been given.

☆ Have the next student chant, "Circle, circle, round the circle."

☆ Call out another spelling word and repeat the process. On her turn, each student must either correctly name the next letter in the word or—if the previous student gave the last letter—repeat the chant of "Circle, circle, round the circle." If she doesn't do either one, then she must sit down.

☆ Continue Circle Spelling until all the words have been spelled.

VARIATION

After a word has been spelled, have the next student write the word on the chalkboard. Then have the *next* student (the one after the writer) say the chant.

TEACHER TIP

You can also use this activity to practice skip counting by twos, threes, fours, fives, sixes, and tens. When the count reaches 100, the next person says the chant.

GRADES: *1–6*
GROUP SIZE: *whole group*

WHEN TO USE: *during spelling review*
FOCUS: *spelling*

Stair-Step Spellers

Rather than reinforcing a particular list of spelling words, this activity builds and strengthens thinking skills while providing an opportunity for spelling sight-word practice.

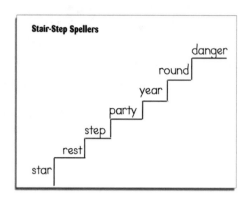

MATERIALS

Stair-step reproducible (see page 101)

Plain white copier paper

Pencils

PREPARATION

Make one copy of the reproducible for each student.

STEP BY STEP

☆ Divide students into pairs or groups of four. Hand out the copies of the reproducible.

☆ Give all groups the same starting word and ask all students to write it on the first stair.

☆ Have the first student in each group come up with a word that everyone in the group can write on the second step. The new word must begin with the last or next-to-the-last letter of the first word.

☆ Ask the next student in each group to repeat the process by coming up with a new word that all group members can write on the third step, still following the same rule. This student is building from the word on the second step.

☆ Students continue taking turns building words in this way until their work resembles a set of word stairs going across and up the paper.

VARIATIONS

Encourage students to practice this activity in a center or learning station.

Instead of the work sheet, use the chalkboard, class whiteboard, and overhead projector as work areas for the student groups.

TEACHER TIP

We recommend giving a copy of the reproducible to each student, even though they're working in pairs or small groups. Every student writes on his copy the words his group comes up with, and every member of the group turns in his copy. If you ask for only one copy of the list from each group, it's too easy for some students to let others do all the work.

Stair-Step Spellers

Basketball Spelling

With this fresh take on a favorite game, students boost their understanding of both spelling and meaning. They practice eye/hand coordination as well.

MATERIALS

2 chairs

2 individual-size whiteboards or chalkboards

Markers or chalk

Masking tape

1 average-size, clean wastebasket or bucket

1 small foam basketball

PREPARATION

Set up the room by placing the two chairs side by side at the front of the room, facing the class, with a board and a marker or piece of chalk on each chair. Place a four-foot length of masking tape on the floor to create a line approximately three feet in front of the two chairs. Divide the desks to separate the class into two teams, with an aisle down the middle. Place the wastebasket in the aisle, approximately ten to fifteen feet in front of the tape. For scorekeeping purposes, list the teams on the classroom chalkboard.

STEP BY STEP

☆ One student from each team comes to the front of the class, sits in one of the chairs, and places the board and writing implement on her lap.

☆ You call out a spelling word.

☆ Each of the two participating players attempts to spell the word correctly on her individual board.

☆ Each student holds up her board. If she's spelled the word correctly, her team receives a point, and she has two more chances to earn additional points.

☆ First, she may try to "make a basket." She stands behind the taped line, being careful not to step over it, and throws the ball in an attempt to get it in the wastebasket. If she succeeds, she receives one additional point and a chance to earn one more.

☆ The next challenge for that same student is to use the word correctly in a sentence. You judge the accuracy of the sentence, and the team receives a third point if the sentence is correct.

☆ When the student isn't able to spell the word, misses the basket, or can't use the word correctly in a sentence, the round ends for that team. The student goes back to her seat, and the next member of the same team comes to one of the front seats, ready for the next round.

☆ Repeat the process.

☆ On the classroom chalkboard, keep track of all points scored.

☆ Continue play until everyone has had a turn.

☆ The team with the most points wins.

GRADES: *2–6*
GROUP SIZE: *whole group*

WHEN TO USE: *during spelling*
FOCUS: *spelling & determining meaning*

VARIATION

Instead of having them create a sentence for each word, ask each student to define the word, tell how many syllables it has, what vowel sounds it contains, etc.

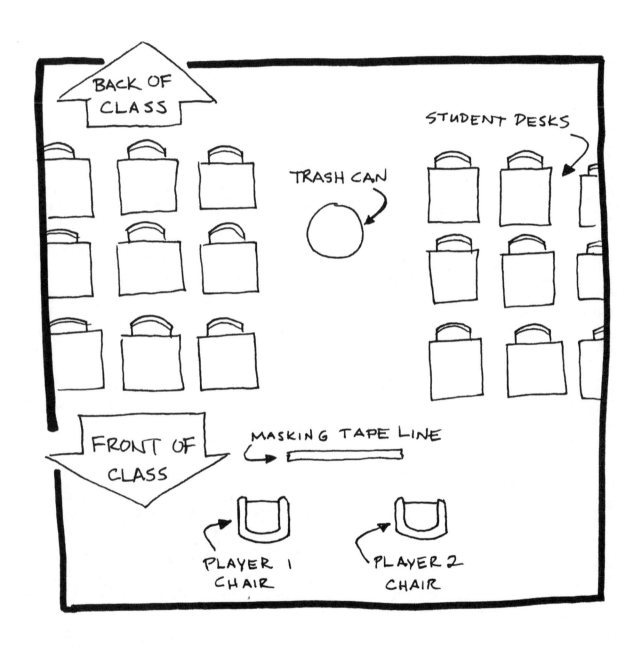

Echo Spelling

A traditional vinyl P-trap (typically used in plumbing) helps students imprint spelling words into their overall schema of words.

MATERIALS

List of spelling words

One 1 ½" P-trap per primary student *or* one 2" P-trap per intermediate student

STEP BY STEP

☆ After introducing spelling words and working with them, allow students time each day to spell the words into the P-trap "phones" while they listen with the other end.

☆ Explain that each student should recite the word and then spell it into the "phone," repeating the process several times for each word.

☆ Encourage students to whisper their work. The sound through the phones will be too loud if they speak in their normal voices. Whispering allows all the students to be echo spelling at the same time.

☆ The connection between speaking and hearing the spelling will imprint the words in the student's memory.

VARIATIONS

Use Echo Spelling as Echo Fact Retention to help students remember definitions or key concepts in content.

Have students recite addition, subtraction, or multiplication facts into the P-trap phones.

TEACHER TIP

P-traps can generally be found in the plumbing section of a hardware store. Or you can substitute phonics phones, available from Crystal Springs Books (www.crystalsprings.com).

GRADES: *1–6*
GROUP SIZE: *individual*

WHEN TO USE: *during spelling*
FOCUS: *spelling retention*

Using Your Noodle for Spelling

When students use macaroni letters to construct words, they work those words into long-term memory, and you get a quick assessment of each child's understanding.

MATERIALS

1 clipboard

List of spelling words

Plain white paper

1 sheet of dark-colored construction paper for each student

Tape

¼ cup measure

2 large bags of alphabet macaroni

1 pencil with an eraser for each student

PREPARATION

Prepare a clipboard with a checklist that includes each child's name and the words to be spelled. Tape a sheet of the construction paper to the top of each child's desk. Using the measuring cup, scoop one quarter-cup of the alphabet macaroni onto the construction paper.

STEP BY STEP

☆ Call out a spelling word.

☆ Have each child attempt to spell the word using the alphabet macaroni. Because these letters are small, you might want to suggest to students that they manipulate the letters with the erasers on their pencils.

☆ Give the students ample time, then check spelling for accuracy.

☆ Mark on the clipboard checklist whether each student spelled the word correctly.

☆ Repeat for each other word on the list.

VARIATIONS

Rather than calling out words, call out the definitions.

Give word clues. For example, for the word "sunshine" you might say, "This is a compound word with two vowel sounds. Both parts of the word begin with the same letter."

To save time, encourage students to organize their letters, pulling out vowels and common consonants and placing them in piles.

GRADES: *2–6*
GROUP SIZE: *whole group with students working individually*

WHEN TO USE: *during spelling*
FOCUS: *spelling*

Matchbook Spelling

Creating a "matchbook" out of spelling words gives students a booklet from which to study.

MATERIALS

One 8 ½" X 11" sheet of colored card stock for every 2 students

One 3" X 8 ½" strip of plain paper per student per word

Colored pencils, markers, or crayons

List of spelling words

Magazines with pictures (optional)

Computer and printer (optional)

Stapler

PREPARATION

Take each sheet of card stock and cut it in half vertically, so you have two sheets that measure 4 ¼" X 11". Take each of these half sheets and fold one short end up approximately one inch from the edge. The goal is to create a flap like a matchbook flap, so the card stock becomes the "matchbook." Hand each student one 3" X 8 ½" strip of paper for each spelling word on the list; if the students have ten spelling words, each student would receive ten 3" X 8 ½" strips. Also give each student one "matchbook" and an assortment of colored pencils, markers, or crayons.

STEP BY STEP

☆ Students place their spelling lists on their desks for reference.

☆ Each student writes one spelling word on each strip of paper. He can write the word in a particular color to help him remember it. He can add magazine pictures, clip art from the computer, or his own drawings. He can write key words or clues around his word. In short, the student is to include on that word strip anything that will help him to remember the word.

☆ After completing that process for each of the ten words, each student places his word strips in a stack and slides the stack down into the folded card-stock flap.

☆ Each student staples his sheets into the flap about one-half inch from the end, then tucks the other end of the card stock into the flap to create a matchbook.

☆ When students use the matchbooks to study their spelling words, the pictures, color, and/or other clues help them to remember the correct spellings.

VARIATIONS

Have students add a definition to each strip of paper.

Ask them to glue on letters cut from magazines instead of writing the words.

Let students use stencils to create the words.

GRADES: *2–6*
GROUP SIZE: *individual*

WHEN TO USE: *during spelling*
FOCUS: *spelling & determining meaning*

Puzzle Power

This spelling game entices the puzzle solvers in your class to put their jigsaw know-how to work while they practice spelling.

MATERIALS

1 jigsaw puzzle with frame for each student, each puzzle containing 8–15 pieces (depending on grade level)

1 plastic bag for each puzzle

List of 8–15 spelling words

1 sheet of notebook paper for each student

Pencils

PREPARATION

Place the pieces and frame of each puzzle in a separate plastic bag.

TEACHER TIP

Make sure there are as many words on the list as there are pieces in the puzzle; if the puzzle has fifteen pieces, the list should have fifteen words. All students should be working with the same list of words and should have the same number of puzzle pieces. Each kindergartener might have eight pieces, each first grader might have ten to twelve pieces, and each second or third grader might have fifteen pieces.

STEP BY STEP

☆ Give each student a plastic bag containing one unsolved puzzle and its frame.

☆ Ask each student to work independently at his seat with a sheet of notebook paper, a pencil, and the puzzle frame in front of him.

☆ Call out one spelling word from the list.

☆ Have each student write the word on his sheet of paper.

☆ Check for accuracy by having one student spell the word aloud as the others check their work.

☆ Explain that each student who's spelled the word correctly may take one piece of the puzzle from his bag and place it in the center of his puzzle frame. Add that he's not to put the puzzle piece in place at this time. (Letting students put the puzzles together as they receive the pieces would place the focus on the puzzle rather than on spelling the words.)

☆ Continue until all the words have been spelled and every child has all the pieces of his puzzle piled in the center of his puzzle frame. (If a student is struggling, you might want to spell the word and then have him spell it after you.)

☆ Give students five minutes to put their puzzles together. Since the students have not seen the puzzle assembled beforehand, this is a fun and challenging activity with the flavor and excitement of a race.

GRADES: *K–3*
GROUP SIZE: *whole group*

WHEN TO USE: *during skills groups*
FOCUS: *spelling*

Buddies for Study

All the varied practice from this activity will generate many perfect papers when you give the weekly spelling test. Besides, students who use this study-with-a-buddy approach every day become more responsible, prepared learners.

MATERIALS

1 file folder for each student

1 sheet of lined paper for each student

Glue

Scissors

List of spelling words

1 wipe-off marker for each student

PREPARATION

The goal is to create a flip book from a file folder. Start by positioning a folder horizontally (with the fold at the bottom), opening it, and gluing a sheet of lined paper to the bottom half of the opened folder. Then, with the folder still open, laminate the bottom half of it (the part where you glued the lined paper). Crease the folder along its original fold. Cut the top half of the folder (the unlaminated part) into thirds, creating three flaps to lift up. Repeat for each of the other folders. Write the week's spelling words on the board and give each child a list of those same words to take home.

TEACHER TIP

It's helpful to list on the outside of each folder what the student is to do on each day of this activity.

STEP BY STEP

☆ Early in the year, divide the class into pairs of "spelling buddies." For twenty minutes every day, these buddies will work together on spelling activities, check each other's work, and erase their own work after completing the day's assignment.

☆ On the first day of a new spelling unit, each student gets a folder and a marker, then meets with her spelling buddy. Each student copies the new list of words from the board, writing it under the first flap of her own folder.

☆ Next, each student practices by closing the first flap and rewriting the words under the second flap. Buddies trade folders, check each other's work, then return the folders to their original owners. Each student takes any words that she spelled incorrectly and rewrites them under the third flap. Then everyone erases everything ex-

cept what's under
the first flap.

☆ The next day, bud-
dies review the
lists under the first
flap together. Each
student works with
her own folder and writes under the second flap
a word that begins or ends in the same way as
each word under the first flap. Buddies discuss
their answers with each other.

☆ Under the third flap, students write a rhyming
word or another word
that reminds them of
each new word they're
studying. Then everyone
again erases everything
except what's under the
first flap.

☆ On the third day, the
buddies look together at the list of words under
the first flap. Each student scrambles the letters
of each word and writes the scrambled versions
under the second flap; then the buddies trade
folders.

☆ On the fourth day, buddies quiz each other on
this week's list, with each student writing her
answers under the second flap of her folder.
Buddies check each other's work, and each
rewrites under the third flap of her own folder
any words she misspelled. Once again, buddies finish by erasing everything except what's
under the first flap

☆ Each buddy tries to solve her partner's scrambled words, writing the answers under the third
flap. Then students check each other's work.

VARIATIONS

Use the same strategy for reading-vocabulary
words.

Use this process to reinforce content vocabulary.

Index

Note: *Page numbers in italics refer to reproducibles to be used with activities.*

Note: *Page numbers in italics refer to reproducibles to be used with activities.*

Note: Page numbers in italics refer to reproducibles to be used with activities.